Resist!

Against a precarious future

Edited by Ray Filar

Part of the Radical Future series
Series editor: Ben Little

Lawrence & Wishart, London 2015

Lawrence and Wishart Limited
99a Wallis Road
London
E9 5LN

Typesetting: e-type
Cover design: Yoav Segal

ISBN 978 1 910448 137

British Library Cataloguing in Publication Data.
A catalogue record for this book is available from the British Library.

CONTENTS

Preface – *Ben Little*   7

Introduction: What the fuck is to be done? – *Ray Filar*   9

Work

1. Re-imagining the future of work – *Rhiannon Colvin*   16
2. Young people and employment: challenging Workfare and dead end jobs – *Craig Berry*   26
3. Plan F and the care crisis: why we need feminist economics – *Polly Trenow*   35

Activism

4. Communities of defence: legal political organising after the riots – *Wail Qasim*   42
5. Resisting the housing crisis – *Mike Shaw and Sean Farmelo*   51
6. Focus E15 mums and the Aylesbury occupation – *Izzy Köksal*   67

Participation

7. Scotland's referendum and the politics of the future – *Niki Seth-Smith*   75
8. Breaking the first rule of generation Y – *Adam Ramsay*   85
9. What would a better democracy look like? – *Sarah Allan*   91

Environment

10. What the frack? Resurgent environmentalism in the UK – *Robbie Gillett*   99
11. Securing the environment's future – *Matt Adam Williams*   107

Media

12. Going mainstream: counterculture and alternative media – *Deborah Grayson*   114
13. The selfish generation: anxiety and belonging in a digital world – *Noel Hatch*   129
14. Who groks Spock? Emotion in the neoliberal market – *Matthew Cheeseman*   134

Acknowledgements

We would like to thank: our contributors, all of whom gave their time for free, cover artist Yoav Segal, former editor Clare Coatman for her fantastic advice, Katharine Harris and Becky Luff of our publishers Lawrence and Wishart, who worked overtime to get this book out before the election, the broader *Radical Future* collective and everybody who contributed to our crowd-funder.

With special thanks to Nina Power, David Williams and Jonah Winch for their generous support which helped us to get the book published.

Preface

It is a sign of how far the conversation has moved on, that since the initial book in this series, the idea of generational politics has become commonplace. We all know what the opinion pieces say by now. Disgruntled gen-Yers bitch and moan about the excesses of baby boomers. We shout about how we want our future back from the greedy bastards who have hoarded away our share in society in gold-plated pension funds and five bedroom houses. Meanwhile, columnists of our parents' age write about how no-one appreciates the challenges of caring for elderly grandparents while supporting those good-for nothing twenty- to forty(!)-somethings who still can't afford to leave home.

This media cliché tells a good story, but it's a false one. It turns a set of difficult social changes into a familial conflict within the broadsheet reading classes. The reality is more complex and this book, like its predecessors, captures that complexity. Not only is there critique of the current moment, articulated passionately by Ray Filar in their introduction, but there are also alternatives to dominant discourses, new directions in action and activism and the possibility of a different political reality to be found in this book's pages. And that's the key thing, because this isn't about petulant young people coveting their parents' wealth; it's about the need for new solutions (and reclaiming old wisdom) to tackle the social, political, economic and environmental problems that neoliberalism either ignores or exacerbates.

And here's the rub. This book, this series of books, shouldn't have to exist. Generational politics should be an irrelevance. Any society that has its eye on survival nurtures its young, and stewards those institutions that effectively support the lives of its citizens, so that struggles do not have to be repeated and lives improve with each generation. Politically, we seem to have forgotten that. One by one, many of our enclaves of social justice, born from the traumas of the nineteenth and twentieth centuries, are being dismantled or destroyed.

The NHS? Up for sale. Co-ops? A target for vulture funds. Education? If you can afford it. Jobs? Maybe, but don't expect a real contract.

Neoliberal capitalism has broken the intergenerational bonds that enable society to continue in a way that is humane, just and sustainable. It is a politics that arrests the possibility of progress towards ever-greater human flourishing and leaves us all diminished. Books like this are important not just for their analysis and ideas, but for their energy: they inspire us to imagine a better future and, when confronted by the brutality of the present moment, they exhort us to resist.

Ben Little
Series Editor

What the fuck is to be done?

Ray Filar

Our generation aren't apathetic, we are angry. Over the last five years the government has mounted an all-out assault on our capacity to live. With homes, communities and jobs unavailable or insecure, precariousness is the new norm. *Resist! Against a precarious future* charts young peoples' collective organisation against this model. It documents our efforts to create a shared, better future.

Despite their conservative rhetoric, this coalition government has taken just one electoral term to enact the most extreme shift in British politics since Thatcher. Our imperatively social, surveilled and alienated generation have been perfect test subjects, trained to deify work, competition, and profit. The government's systemic transfer of wealth and property to the rich is a well-documented part of neoliberalism, as is the wholesale privatisation of institutions, like the NHS or social security, formerly held in common. Following in Tony Blair's footsteps, in this way Cameron and co have successfully honed Thatcher's project to an art form.

Their outsourcing-for-profit of public goods has at its core a more malignant aim – to target the public itself. But perhaps their greatest success has been the attack on hope. By deliberately appealing to fear, resentment, our basest emotions, they have manufactured a climate of suspicion aimed at those who suffer most. Policy to entrench inequality contains within itself the naturalisation of that inequality: the poor become poor by their own hands, minorities are marginalised by their own design. The irony is that this government are the ones who bandy around the term 'extremist'. They don't acknowledge their own hypocrisy.

Those of us who don't believe that this is freedom are pushed to accept it as political pragmatism, as inevitability, as the kind of 'tough decisions' that the manly 'muscular liberals' in government excel at.

But they forgot that their impact is keenly personally felt, particularly (though not exclusively) by the post-1979 millennial generation reaching adulthood under this new, intensified regime. When another of my friends tells me that they can't leave the house today, that they feel too anxious or despairing to face benefits appointments, that they can't face another shift at the call centre, when apathy or intoxicants feel like the best or only solution, it gives fuel to the backlash against this powerlessness. Our resistance opens up new possibilities: we can refocus the lens back on those who pretend this isn't of their creation. It isn't just that mainstream politics has failed us. We know that it was never for us.

In the run up to the 2015 general election, *Resist!* emerges from two premises: that mainstream party politics is obsolete to many, and broken to many more – despite its continued control over how we live – and that the traditional institutions of the UK left are failing to put forward a persuasive alternative. The group of young(ish) activists, writers, artists and academics involved in the *Radical Future* collective first thought of this – the third book in the series – as a renewed intervention into this dangerous political stagnation. We want it to stand as a rebuttal to the flaccid calls from centrist think-tanks and campaign groups to 'get young people involved', as a kick-back against the short-termism of the electoral cycle, and as a positive elaboration of our shared belief in social justice, liberation and collectivity (and for some: full communism). Of course, there is no need to reinvent the wheel; through these pages we draw on a history of left political action and thought. Yet in aiming this book at other young people, we hope to speak to those who do not feel Marx is for them, or who may not be part of direct action groups, or who may not yet have found ways to express their frustration with the current moment. We don't all advocate for the same thing, but all of us continue to believe in realisable, radical alternatives to neoliberalism and precarity, anxiety and disempowerment.

It can be tempting to imagine that active resistance had died out by mid-2012, as the much-hyped wave of global uprisings petered out, as they failed to achieve their demands, or – as in Egypt – were co-opted and reversed. The militarised, late-capitalist state doesn't just clamp down brutally on collective action, its cultural outlets also stigmatise empathy with disadvantaged groups: mocking those who protest, defining them as 'lunatics', 'idealists' or 'violent anarchists'. As **Noel**

Hatch documents in his chapter, a 2013 Ipsos Mori study found that our generation – growing up in a digital, globalised era – are less supportive of welfare spending than any other generation.[1] These kinds of trends have led some to characterise us as 'the selfish generation'. If they have us right, we are individualist, consumerist machines, interested, supposedly, only in commercial success and our personal brands (see: selfies). This makes us an obvious target audience: defenceless against the 'pull-yourself-up-by-the-bootstraps' coalition propaganda on the merits of hard work and 'doing the right thing'. And as Hatch argues, though digital globalisation challenges traditionally imagined social structures – the nation-state, the patriarchal nuclear family – opening up space to re-imagine belonging and affinity, it also leaves us unbounded, unsure of whether we identify with anybody else at all. This impedes our opposition, specifically our ability to organise around solidarity or shared experience.

Perhaps individualisation is an inevitability, growing up under the neoliberal settlement. As **Matthew Cheeseman** writes, thinking through the figure of *Star Trek*'s Spock, today science and logic are rarely challenged as final arbiters of truth. But the ideals that politicians dress up as logic persuade through the appeal to peoples' emotions and desires, often mobilising prejudice under the guise of fact. Today the 'invisible hand' of the market might be analysed as having become sentient, he suggests, capable of making claims about the public good, common sense, and human nature. How could we help but absorb some of the attitudes of the time in which we live? What we're missing, he says, is a sense of collectivity: we need this combined generational confidence to reclaim knowledge of ourselves and others from the market.

Even so, a key theme emerged in the chapters: continued active resistance. Despite trivialising media coverage, between 2010 and 2012, protest felt both necessary and viable. Stunned by the immediate violence of a Conservative party with just 36 per cent of the vote, we fought back. Predominantly middle class students, who often hadn't had to think twice about how politics affected our lives, became involved. The student movement, alongside the 2011 London riots over the killing of Mark Duggan, mobilised the greatest numbers of any action since those against the Iraq War. But unlike the student protests, the riots were led predominantly by young people of colour and young working-class people, and they conspicuously led to mass arrests. 2000 people were found guilty of riot-related offences, including, memorably, the rioter who was imprisoned for six months for stealing a case of bottled water worth £3.50. As **Wail Qasim** argues in his chapter, people – including many on the white, middle-class left – queued up to denounce the rioters as consumerist looters, a race and class privileged decrial that could only be made by 'those sure of their own security under capitalism'. Considering legal defence organising after the riots, Qasim asks: how have left activist organisers and community organisers resisted the brutality of the law and state violence since then? We should look to the current Ferguson protests and 'I can't breathe' movements sweeping the United States, which position black life in opposition to the law. This might enable us to turn towards vitality, the importance of life, in our activism.

For those who see elections as more than an irrelevance, this year's marks a departure from the norm. While the 2014 Scottish referendum posed a credible threat to 'Britain', the failings of Westminster's two-party system have never been so apparent. **Niki Seth-Smith** argues that the referendum was the most important political event yet for our generation. She reflects on its radical potential, and what it means for young peoples' relationships with a politics of nationhood: what can we learn from the 'Yes' campaign's successful mobilisation of 80 per cent of the youth vote? Arguing in favour of involvement in radical politics more generally, **Adam Ramsay** also notes what he sees as a resurgence of interest in joining political groups. Noting 'the Green surge' – since 2010 the combined Green parties' membership has gone from 10,000 to 63,000 – he examines the myriad reasons behind our generation's seeming reluctance to participate. He argues that single-issue campaigns are no longer enough, that we need long-term institutions that can tackle interconnected problems, whether these are political parties or activist groups.

This book is a partial catalogue of resistance, a documenting of how the young have organised in the face of precarity, austerity, and anxiety. Given the failure of the mainstream media to take us seriously, to even report on our protest movements, we are archiving our own activism and political engagement. Quite evidently this archive is not exhaustive, neither is it representative of the range of young people's work – rather it gives a series of snapshots from the perspectives of the contributors: flashes of radical potential within mass movements, of the continued strength of grassroots actions. So while speaking of collectivity or of hope, we offer up some practiced examples of it. In this we build on the work of the two previous books in the series, *Regeneration* and *Radical Future: Politics for the next generation*. As Clare Coatman and Guy Shrubsole wrote in their introduction to *Regeneration*: 'We are beginning to tell our own story'. In this sense, we are starting to do what **Deborah Grayson** argues for in her *Resist!* chapter: we are building a counter-narrative in an attempt to circumvent the 'symbolic centre', the place occupied and controlled by legacy media. Looking at the problems faced by alternative media like Indymedia and openDemocracy, and the comparatively successful awareness-raising undertaken by the Palestine solidarity movement, Grayson concludes that institutions, and money, will be crucial to our ability to represent ourselves.

Precarity plays out generationally: many of us are paying more than half our wages in rent, living in atrocious housing, without any prospects of future ownership. **Mike Shaw and Sean Farmelo** explain the formation of the British housing crisis and its impact on young people. While millions of people are in need of homes, less than half the amount needed are built per year. This is not accidental, they say, rather it is the direct effect of three decades of government policy intended at increasing profits for the already-wealthy. They also discuss the process of setting up Edinburgh's Student Housing Co-operative, which houses 106 people. To concentrate too much on our insecurity is also to erase our capacity for everyday resistance. **Izzy Köksal** reports on recent direct action housing struggles against local councils' 'regeneration' campaigns, in which tenants are removed from social housing for the purposes of gentrification. She documents the successes of young activist groups like Focus E15 mums, who under the slogan 'social housing not social cleansing', successfully defeated Newham council's attempt to rehouse them outside London. She also discusses the challenges facing the squatters who have been occupying the South London Aylesbury estate since early 2015. Groups like the E15 mums suggest that we are seeing the beginning of a radical new housing movement in London.

Though the anti-austerity movement may have died down by 2012, it gave rise to a new wave of environmental activism. **Robbie Gillett** tracks the resurgence of UK environmentalism, concentrating on the anti-fracking actions carried out by activist groups 'Frack Off' and 'Reclaim the Power', specifically at Balcombe and Barton Moss.

'Situating environmental concerns within a wider left framework of social inequality and corporate dominance remains key', he argues. Young people will be growing old with the consequences of the destruction of the natural environment, says **Matt Adam Williams**. While wildlife is increasingly at risk, he says, young peoples' connection to it is at its lowest ever point. His chapter is a homage to the importance of natural conservation; the emerging community of young conservationists could become a movement akin to the youth climate change movement.

Resist! also puts forward solutions: there is an alternative; we see it happening. **Polly Trenow** explores the care crisis, in which the responsibility of care for children, the elderly, sick and disabled continues to fall on women (predominantly those who are working class, of colour and/or migrants). We need a feminist economy, she says, in which care is revalued, becoming seen as a necessity. Being a carer should not impede on our quality of life or economic prospects. One problem with the electoral system is that it claims to be representative and accountable, when it is not. **Sarah Allan** argues for a participatory democracy that offers people the chance to be involved in political decision-making in between elections.

Anybody who has been on the dole knows that jobs are hard-contested, scarce and depressing. At the end of 2014, 15 per cent of eighteen to twenty-four year-olds were unemployed. This should be understood as a response to the emergence of the low-wage, services-led economy, says **Craig Berry.** The individualisation of employment gives rise to 'zero hours' contracts, phony self-employment and chronic job insecurity. The real purpose of the government's 'Work Programme' (aka 'Workfare') is to intimidate those *in* work into reconsidering their expectations. We need a new political economy of work, with radical trade unionism at its heart. As the founder of a workers' cooperative that supports young people to set up co-operatives, **Rhiannon Colvin** argues that the young should be central to creating change in the labour market. Our generation can organise to set up worker co-operatives and freelancers' unions. But a radically different future of work also requires structural change: a shorter working week and a guaranteed basic income for everyone would, she says – as well as strengthening the economy – put an end to one half of the population being overworked and stressed, while the other half is unemployed and depressed.

Putting together a collective book for free, while not at work, or while coping with cycles of poor mental health, leads to problems. Our contributors are predominantly white and university-educated. While there is a much better gender balance than in the previous two books, *Resist!* is still male-dominated. And of course the content reflects this. It is true to some extent that time and resource constraints lead to commissioning those people who are known on a particular topic, and who have the unusually privileged capacity to write for free. Of course, we are immensely grateful to our contributors for their kindly donated time, work and ideas. In saying this I don't wish to justify or explain away a failure to commission more broadly, but rather to call attention to the limitations of our combined demographic. The *Radical Future* collective would love to hear from other writers who may be interested in involvement in future projects.

What does it mean to stand against a precarious future? Our insecurity gives rise to society-wide anxiety. For many it is deeply felt, experienced in/on the body, through waves of despair or nausea or psychosis. Yet our resistance is political and structural, and personal and affective. Mental ill-health can be a form of political refusal, or political resistance in itself. What we're calling for is collective organisation, for community, for a set of shared political values, and an end to the short-termism of the five-year electoral cycle. In *Resist!* we hope to show that while the global wave of protest may have subsided, for now, young people's attempts to create change are far from over. Despite the litany of obstacles thrown at us, despite the challenges to our mental and physical well-being, we are organising. We won't take this lying down.

Ray Filar is a Contributing Editor at openDemocracy magazine, working on the Transformation section. Their freelance journalism has been published in *The Guardian*, *The Times*, the *Times Literary Supplement* and the *New Statesman*, among others. Ray is interested in intersectional politics and queer subcultures. They tweet from @rayfilar.

Note

1. http://www.ipsos-mori-generations.com/

Re-imagining the future of work

Rhiannon Colvin

Imagine that it's 2025 and the world of work has changed. Today, we do labour out of passion, not obligation. Nobody has a low-paid job or has to balance multiple jobs just to make rent. Work gives us meaning and direction, but it does not define who we are. The three-day working week means we have time to spend with friends and family, to contribute to our communities and have a say in how society in run.

There is no unpaid intern working for a boss on a six-figure salary; one person is not paid ten times another. Pay is allocated equally and fairly depending on the time and skills each person has contributed that month. Holiday and sick pay are mandatory. Everybody has input into how the organisation is run. Colleagues are equal: when decisions are made they are made together. The profit a company makes gets shared between the people who make it possible – the workers, not some distant shareholders. In this labour market, competition and inequality is reduced, and so are the feelings of injustice and worthlessness felt by many.

This new economy is directed towards solving social and environmental problems rather than creating them. Companies focus on protecting the rainforest rather than destroying it, on creating renewable energy rather than drilling more oil out of the ground, on making technologies that empower communities rather than companies, on building affordable and sustainable housing rather than expensive city apartments. The creative energy of musicians, artists and designers is directed towards helping people overcome addiction, inspiring youth, exploring ideas, generating debate or building community, not towards advertising and encouraging people to buy things they do not need, or making them feel inadequate.

In 2025 work generates a fair income, enables us to do what we love and to have a positive impact. Our economy is based upon principles of democracy, equality, sharing and sustainability.

But in 2015, this seems like a utopian dream. It would require a complete overhaul of the system in which we currently live. Could our actions create such a future?

Who will make change happen?

There are limits to the change we can create without a widespread redistribution of wealth and power in the economy. Prior to the overthrow and reconfiguration of the state, there are already a number of existing proposals for how we could create work that is more equal and fulfilling. This chapter will consider four: worker co-operatives, the three-day working week, basic income and freelancers' unions. The young generation has the capacity to push for these kinds of radical changes. But how would we get there from our current situation?

Co-operatives

A co-operative business is a specific type of organisation, one which is run and owned by workers, rather than stock market shareholders. In a co-operative, workers have an equal say over how the business is run as well as an equal share of the profits. Co-operatives reshape the social and environmental impact of our labour, and the way in which we work together to achieve it. Contrary to the idea of the ruthless individual entrepreneur portrayed in television shows like *The Apprentice*, they offer a supportive and collaborative model of entrepreneurship that is about working together to improve society, not fighting to be the best and sole person at the top. At least in principle, co-operatives aim to create both an economy directed towards positive social and environmental change, and one that is more equal and democratic.

In 2012, I was one of the many graduates leaving university and entering the world of work. I had heard about youth unemployment, about how competitive the 'graduate market' was, but I had a good degree, work experience and had spent time volunteering. I thought I would be fine. How wrong I was. I applied endlessly for jobs, but eventually had to move back home, going back to the waitressing job I had before university. During this time I got an interview for an unpaid internship at a youth organisation in London. Whilst undergoing the rigorous assessment process to see whose free labour the charity would choose, I asked how many other young people had applied for this position. The answer: 150.

This was a 'light bulb moment'. 150 young people applying for one unpaid placement, supposedly to empower other young people ... what was going on? This got me thinking, how can we stop competing and start co-operating to create change in a way that enables us to also survive?

I started an organisation called AltGen,[1] that supports young people to set up co-operative businesses as a collaborative solution to youth unemployment, as well as a practical way to build a more equal and sustainable economy that we can be in control of. We provide start up grants, business advice and mentoring to help young people start co-ops, as well as running educational workshops and campaigning on a national and European level.

Worldwide, 1 billion people are already members of a co-operative. That's one seventh of the world's population.[2] There are over 6000 co-operative businesses in the UK. They also exist in all sectors of the economy: there are co-operative schools, art galleries, web design agencies, architects, construction firms, doctors' surgeries and record labels. The central point is the workers have an equal say over how the business is run, equal share of the profit, and care about the impact of their work on people and the planet.

For our generation co-operatives can combine the freedom of freelancing, of being your own boss (choosing who you work for and when) with the security, support, workers' rights and benefits that are supposed to accrue to employees in a traditional business. Co-operatives can change our experience of work in the here and now, and redistribute power and wealth generated through business activity. Yet it is important to acknowledge that the co-operatives still function within the current capitalist economic paradigm: on their own they are not a significant enough threat to fundamentally change the system.

Setting up co-operative businesses is one way that our generation can begin to change the nature of work right now. We can choose to co-operate instead of compete; to do something we love instead of something we hate; to have a say over our work; and a fair share of the profit.

Universal Basic Income

Universal Basic Income (UBI) is the idea that every citizen – regardless of employment, earnings, age or gender – should receive a guaranteed minimum income from the state: a single weekly or monthly monetary payment with no stipulations as to how it, or the time of its recipients, is spent.

This idea is gaining traction around the world and across the political spectrum. It has been argued for from left, liberal and communist perspectives by the likes of Stuart White,[3] as a way to alleviate poverty, to ensure all citizens' basic needs are met and to significantly reduce inequality. The Equality Trust suggest it will reduce crime and mental illness, and improve levels of health and education.[4] On the other end of the spectrum, even right wing economists like Charles Murray support it,[5] for reasons linked to increasing entrepreneurial activity and decreasing state bureaucracy.

It is a core policy of the Green Party in the UK,[6] and it recently went to referendum in Switzerland[7] – a process that requires over 100,000 signatures. In the Swiss example, every adult would receive 2500 Swiss Francs a month, equivalent to £1725. The Green party proposal suggests £72 a week per person, equivalent to the current weekly Jobseekers' Allowance for over twenty-fives.

The theory is that UBI enables all citizens to at least meet their basic needs. UBI would replace the current means-tested state benefits model. It could create help to create a new landscape for the labour market.

Firstly, UBI would reduce the likelihood of people remaining stuck in a poverty trap. Since the 2008 financial crisis it has become increasingly impossible to survive on wage labour. In real terms, wages in the UK have declined 9 per cent in the last five years,[8] whilst in the same period the cost of living has risen 25 per cent.[9] Mass unemployment and the reduction of state welfare support have also taken their toll on our ability to survive.[10] Whether in or out of work, poverty is a reality for millions of people living in the UK, despite the fact that we live in the world's sixth largest economy.

Secondly, it would give people greater freedom to choose work that they are actually interested in and passionate about: a choice based on desire rather than necessity. Many people do jobs they hate just to survive, just as many people know there is no point to the work they do, as David Graeber highlights in his writing on 'bullshit jobs'.[11] Creative potential and talent is being wasted, as people struggle to survive, rather than contributing to the development and progression of society.

Critics of UBI suggest that it would lead to people doing no work at all. But experiments with basic income schemes in North America and Namibia have shown that not only did most people continue to work, but that it significantly increased entrepreneurial activity and the generation of new ideas.[12] Even Google understand the benefits of allowing the space and freedom for their staff to pursue their own interests. Gmail was invented during '20 per cent time', whereby employees can spend up to 20 per cent of their time doing what they want. Unfortunately the time is harnessed to corporate, capitalist ends: all ideas are owned by Google.

Finally, and importantly, UBI would allow everyone to reap the benefits of the technological advancements of the last 100 years, including working fewer hours. Keynes predicted in the 1930s that by the twenty-first century we would be working fifteen hours per week,[13] yet in the UK today we have the highest working hours in Europe. With the advancement of technology, there has been a decrease in the amount of human labour needed; this is leading to mass job cuts and poverty. UBI and the three-day working week combined would address this issue, leaving us with more free time to spend as we choose.

One valid criticism of UBI is that no-one would want to do the jobs that are not particularly enjoyable and inspiring: working at a check-out till, data entry or cold calling. Many of these jobs are for companies that may not be needed; others that are necessary could be automated where possible. Yet there are also jobs that people may not find enjoyable that are needed for society to function, such as collecting rubbish, driving buses or fixing street lamps. What would be the fairest way to ensure that these essential services are still provided? My suggestion is something similar to national service, a non-militaristic citizens' service that everyone does for one year between college and further education or work. You contribute to society for one year of your life, and know that these things will be provided for the rest of your life. This would potentially have some impact on people's respect for, and solidarity with, the workers doing these jobs.

This is just a suggestion. Divorced from wider social change UBI could too easily be co-opted by the state, becoming corrupt, authoritarian, and nationalistic. In combination with other radical restructuring, it could increase solidarity, respect and a culture of mutual aid in society.

Freelancers' Unions

There are also a number of freelancers' unions and co-operatives being created to provide protection and support specifically for freelance workers. Many of the more traditional trade unions are not structured to support the growing generation of freelancers. But some old unions have adapted, including the UK National Union of Journalists, and new unions are emerging specifically to support freelancers.

In the US, a completely new organisation called the Freelancers Union has been created.[14] It has over 249,000 members and provides health insurance, disability allowance, and pensions as well as campaigning for a 'new form of mutualism' that supports freelance workers being in control, collaborating together and serving the community.

Across Europe, exciting models are emerging too. In Holland there is 'Broodfunds',[15] translated as 'Bread Funds', where a group of self-employed people regularly put money aside to support members that become too ill to work for an extended period. In France freelancers' co-operatives such as Coopaname are being set up to overcome the difficulty of claiming unemployment benefits, as well as to provide additional benefits.[16] Here, in exchange for 10 per cent of your earnings, you can become an employee of the co-op. Coopaname offers business mentoring, advice, space for meetings and a supportive and diverse network of freelancers. SMART,[17] in Belgium, has over 60,000 members, and offers an exchange of similar services, as well as paying and chasing up unpaid invoices on freelancers' behalves.

These different models are trying to deal with the difficulty and isolation of freelance work in a number of different ways: creating a community of support, fighting for fair contracts and pay, collectivising resources to gain the same benefits as employees, and providing services that allow freelancers to focus on their creative work rather than on complex legal issues and on admin.

The Three-Day Working Week

The three-day or shorter working week has become an increasingly popular policy proposal in the aftermath of the economic crisis. It is advocated for by disparate figures, from the world's second richest man, Carlos Slim,[18] to leading medical practitioners.[19] In the UK, many of us spend a majority of our time in work, but research suggests that working twenty-one hours – three days – a week could lead to significant improvements in the economy, human well-being and our impact on the environment.[20]

After the economic crisis the German government encouraged and subsidised companies to trim down working hours rather than jobs,[21] enabling a continuation in consumption and demand, and ensuring that unemployment levels never rose as high as the rest of Europe's. In the UK, a similar shift towards a shorter working week could be implemented gradually, alongside efforts to increase wage levels across the country: campaigns such as The Living Wage are already pushing us in the right direction.[22] The Living Wage campaign was developed after research showed that if you worked the average number of hours a week in the UK (forty), at the minimum wage (£6.50 an hour), which averages to around £12,000 a year, £11,000 after tax, you would not be able to meet your basic needs.[23] It suggests that a minimum wage, which people can actually live on – a living wage. This is currently £7.85 outside of London and £9.15 in London. The campaign has already succeeded in making 100,000 businesses,[24] including many government departments, pay all their employees living wage. A three-day working week paid at living wage at least, alongside UBI, would enable us all to work less.

The most common criticism of the three-day working week is that it would weaken our economy. But many countries where people work fewer hours, such as Germany and the Netherlands, have a stronger and more robust economy than the UK.[25] A three-day working week could help create a more healthy and balanced relationship with work for our generation, as well as a more equal and sustainable economy overall. Research by UK think tank nef suggests that the three-day working week would make our work more productive, that we would no longer have one half of the population overworked and stressed, with the other half unemployed and depressed.[26] A three-day week would give us time to relax, exercise, be with people we love, and reflect upon what we really value in life rather than just work and consume. It could contribute to greater gender equality, as everyone would have time to work and look after children if they so chose, balancing out the amount of undervalued and unpaid labour that women currently do. Finally, it could help us to reduce our carbon footprint, and to ensure that we all have more time to have to engage in politics, locally and nationally, to ask questions and to campaign for change.

Conclusion

The labour market has changed fast, specifically with regard to the atomisation and isolation of workers. Whilst this is supposed to give us greater freedom and control, it actually erodes the rights of workers, which previous generations spent years fighting for. Many young workers today can't even imagine the idea of sick pay, holiday pay, guaranteed hours, set wages, a pension fund.

Not only is a more equal, sustainable and fulfilling future of work possible, it is already being built by people and movements across the world. The economy is anything but stable, and this crisis opens up space for us to create a better future.

Our generation stands at a crossroads: we could continue to accept the crisis we have been handed, fight one another for unpaid work, do jobs that we hate, and work fifty hour weeks. Or, we could refuse to participate in this set up any longer, and we could start creating something different and better. A shorter working week, UBI, workers' co-operatives and freelancers' unions represent four forms of possible radical change: young people can make this happen. It's time to stop competing, and start collaborating, to create the kind of future we want to see.

Rhiannon Colvin graduated two years ago and after competing in the brutal graduate job market and researching solutions to youth unemployment in Portugal and Spain she founded AltGen. AltGen supports eighteen to twenty-nine year olds to set up co-operative businesses as an empowering and collaborative solution to youth unemployment. She believes that if we want to create a more equal and sustainable economy where young people feel ownership and control, we need to stop competing and start co-operating.

Notes

1. www.altgen.org.uk
2. http://www.uk.coop/
3. 'Stuart White. Lecture 1: The communist case for basic income. Part 1'. https://www.youtube.com/watch?v=Kw4jCkXPS-Q
4. *Ibid.*
5. 'The cheque is in the mail', The Economist: Democracy in America blog, 19 November 2013. http://www.economist.com/blogs/democracyinamerica/ 2013/11/government-guaranteed-basic-income

6. Jon Stone, 'Green Party to give "universal income" a front-row seat in its manifesto', BuzzFeed News, 8 August 2014. http://www.buzzfeed.com/jonstone/greens-to-lead-on-universal-basic-income

7. Imogen Foulkes, 'Swiss to vote on incomes for all – working or not', BBC News, 18 December 2013. http://www.bbc.co.uk/news/business-25415501

8. Brian Groom, 'When will the big squeeze on wages end?', *Financial Times*, 6 September 2013. http://www.ft.com/cms/s/0/1abaeafe-161e-11e3-856f-00144feabdc0.html

9. 'A minimum income standard for the UK in 2013', Joseph Rowntree Foundation, 2013. http://www.jrf.org.uk/sites/files/jrf/income-living-standards-summary.pdf

10. Andrew Dolan, 'Do they owe us a living? 7 reasons the Universal Basic Income is worth fighting for', Novaramedia, 19 February 2015. http://wire.novaramedia.com/2014/02/do-they-owe-us-a-living-7-reasons-the-universal-basic-income-is-worth-fighting-for/

11. David Graeber, 'On the phenomenon of bullshit jobs', *Strike! Magazine*, 17 August 2013. http://strikemag.org/bullshit-jobs/

12. Stephen Reid, 'National 20 per cent time', Words and Writing blog, 27 December 2013. http://www.wordsandwriting.me/blog/post/national-20-time

13. Larry Elliott, 'Economics: whatever happened to Keynes' fifteen-hour working week?' *The Guardian*, 1 December 2008. http://www.theguardian.com/business/2008/sep/01/economics

14. https://www.freelancersunion.org/

15. http://www.broodfonds.nl/

16. http://www.coopaname.coop/

17. http://smartbe.be/en/

18. Maria Tedeo, 'Billionaire Carlos Slim calls for three-day working week', *The Independent*, 9 October 2014. http://www.independent.co.uk/news/business/news/billionaire-carlos-slim-calls-for-threeday-working-week-9785768.html

19. Denis Campbell, 'UK needs four-day week to combat stress, says top doctor', *The Guardian*, 1 July 2014. http://www.theguardian.com/society/2014/jul/01/uk-four-day-week-combat-stress-top-doctor

20. Anna Coote, 'Ten reasons for a shorter working week', The NEF blog, 29 July 2014. http://www.neweconomics.org/blog/entry/10-reasons-for-a-shorter-working-week

21. 'Making short work of things', *The Economist*, 4 August 2010. http://www.economist.com/blogs/freeexchange/2010/08/german_recovery

22. http://www.livingwage.org.uk/

23. Shaun Rafferty, 'The minimum wage is not enough – we must aspire to pay a living wage', Joseph Rowntree Foundation blog, 17 April 2013. http://www.jrf.org.uk/blog/2013/04/minimum-wage-living-wage

24. Yvonne Roberts, 'A living wage revolution: how a brave idea become

reality', *The Observer*, 1 November 2014. http://www.theguardian.com/society/2014/nov/01/living-wage-companies-signed-up-doubled

25. Anna Coote, 'Ten reasons for a shorter working week', The NEF blog, 29 July2014.http://www.neweconomics.org/blog/entry/10-reasons-for-a-shorter-working-week

26. *Ibid.*

Young people and employment: challenging Workfare and dead end jobs

Craig Berry

Youth unemployment is one of the clearest indications that young people are suffering more than any other generation from the implications of the 2008 financial crisis, and the subsequent policy responses of Britain's political elite. But an ongoing assault on pay and conditions means that even for many of those young people who are in employment, work can be a miserable experience. We should not assume that these problems are simply the result of the financial crisis; the economic downturn exacerbated trends that were already evident, and that were constitutive of the transformation of the British economy under the stewardship of neoliberalism.

This chapter charts, specifically, how unemployment has been individualised, and demonstrates how young people can collectively fight back. It begins by situating young people's labour market woes within the emergence of a low-wage, services-led economy in Britain, and then offers an account of the real motives behind the coalition government's failing Work Programme and related initiatives. It argues that the path away from this economy, created in neoliberalism's image, will not be found for today's young people by simply adopting a new agenda for labour market policy, but rather by mobilising in support of a new political economy of employment and work, with radical trade unionism at its heart.

Unemployment and young people in post-crisis Britain

In early 2014, George Osborne advocated a return to 'full employment'.[1] Had he, with one rhetorical flourish, reversed several decades of neoliberal labour market orthodoxy? Sadly not. Full employment may once again be considered a public good by Britain's political elite, but this is not the full employment of post-war Keynesian theory, in which providing and enabling decent-paying jobs was crucial to supporting economic growth by boosting consumer demand. Instead, full employment has returned to our political lexicon as moralistic froth. Neoliberal ideology – which vanquished Keynesianism politically in the late 1970s – previously upheld the economic value of unemployment in combating inflation. Yet today, its victory in dismantling workers' rights, and the whole architecture of Keynesian economic statecraft, means that it is rather more comfortable in endorsing full employment as a policy ambition, insofar as it chimes with its longstanding agenda around reducing so-called welfare dependency.

Herein lies the continuity within neoliberal thinking, despite the *volte-face* on full employment. Depressingly, the moral discourse on worklessness that (re)emerged in the 1970s is now part of the 'common sense' of British politics. Being out of work carries extremely negative social connotations, deemed the fault of individuals – so-called skivers and scroungers – rather than a product of the way the labour market is (quite deliberately) structured.[2] Under the Thatcher government, this discourse justified the maintenance of high unemployment – desirable in-itself to restrict wage rises, but also an inevitable consequence of Margaret Thatcher's pursuit of a strong pound, at the behest of the City of London, which helped to decimate British manu-facturing.[3] Under the coalition government (intensifying the New Labour government's agenda), the discourse justifies a relentless assault on out-of-work social security benefits so that individuals are compelled to accept *any* job.

This agenda can be explained with reference to the type of jobs that the British economy now creates, and this is vital to appreciating the employment prospects of today's young people. Britain has undergone a rapid and extensive process of deindustrialisation. It is now utterly dominated by the services sector, which makes up almost 80 per cent of economic output. The champions of services sector employment like to emphasise high-tech industries like telecommunications. The reality, however, is that the transition to services encompasses a vast withdrawal of technology from our economy – even as it encroaches evermore on our daily lives – as heavy industry is replaced by personal, consumer and social services (think gyms, call centres and care homes). These new jobs are 'labour-intense', dependent not on the application of machinery or chemicals, for example, but rather the 'hands on' contribution of actual human beings.[4]

This means the capacity for productivity growth – where the production process becomes more efficient, so more can be produced even if the resources that are input into production remain at the same level – is fairly limited. It is precisely this which means wages must be kept low. The services-led economy needs lots of worker bees, and so cannot retain profitability if earnings rise too much. So the welfare safety net must be as low as possible (most benefit recipients are now in employment, receiving wage top-ups in the form of tax credit), and employment protection diluted as much as possible.

The dominance of the services sector has emerged in tandem with the increasing 'financialisation' of the British economy, dictating a national business model in which incentives for investment are limited, and firms in pursuit of short-term financial gains gravitate towards low-cost industries where very little initial investment or expertise is required in order to set up in business. As suggested above, these industries generate high employment, but as most jobs require only limited skill levels, opportunities for progression and employers' incentives to retain employees are significantly undermined.[5]

The kind of labour market problems associated with this model have been well-documented. As well as low wages, the rise of 'zero hours' contracts demonstrates the normalisation of chronic job insecurity.[6] We have also seen, more recently, enormous growth in phoney self-employment – as companies outsource jobs that would previously been undertaken by formal employees. Many disadvantaged people seek to supplement meagre incomes by offering personal services within their communities, often at rates of pay far below the minimum wage.[7]

Young people are by definition the most adversely affected by such trends. Firstly, such problems are more likely to be experienced by people at the beginning of their career, before their value to employers increases. That is hardly comforting for those on the receiving end, but it at least suggests that the experience will be temporary for most. However, an explanation emphasising the generational specificity of today's young people is less positive – it suggests that currently, young people are the victims of the post-crisis intensification of Britain's low-road national business model, and may be permanently scarred as such.

Yet even this more alarming account fails to fully capture the structural disconnect between young people and today's labour market.

Today's young people might not simply be in the wrong place at the wrong time, but rather, actually the first cohort of young people to fully experience the implications of the UK's industrial transformation. It is worth noting the high value placed on 'soft skills' by services sector employers, developed not only through work experience but also life experience. Simply, people like to be served by people who look and sound a little bit like themselves, and this bias manifests – unfairly – in a widespread mistrust in the competence and courteousness of young people.[8]

This helps to explain the staggeringly high youth unemployment rate in Britain, which was evident before the recession and has remained much higher than the general unemployment rate as the economy has recovered in statistical terms. For eighteen to twenty-four year olds, unemployment stood at around 15 per cent at the end of 2014, having peaked above 20 per cent at the end of 2011. In contrast, the general unemployment rate was around 6 per cent at the end of 2014, having peaked at around 8.5 per cent three years earlier.[9]

Despite constant media discourse around skills shortages, Britain actually has an acute skills under-utilisation problem created by a generation of young people leaving education with all the right qualifications but too few occupations to apply them to.[10] This is the real tragedy of young people in today's labour market, as the failure to utilise their education is not only economically suicidal, but seriously jeopardises a generation's ability to contribute meaningfully to society through work and, ultimately, individuals' sense of self-worth.

The double-edged failure of welfare-to-work

The coalition government has stacked up an impressive number of policy disasters since 2010, but few have been pilloried as much as the Work Programme, the government's flagship welfare-to-work scheme. The Work Programme is a mandatory, two-year programme for people who have been claiming Jobseekers' Allowance (JSA) for more than a year (nine months for young people). Through the scheme, participants are usually offered intense support in searching for work, and basic training in job-acquisition skills such as CV-writing.

Measured by conventional means, the scheme is failing: it is not succeeding in placing the long-term unemployed into sustainable employment. Only 3 per cent of cases have led to providers (who are largely paid by results) being paid in full, as a result of delivering sustainable employment.[11] It is worth noting that Britain spends considerably less than virtually all other European countries on supply-side labour market interventions such as the Work Programme – less than 0.5 per cent of GDP, compared to around 1 per cent in France, Germany, Sweden, Spain and the Netherlands, and around 1.5 per cent in Belgium and Denmark.[12]

From a more critical perspective, however, the Work Programme is performing perfectly adequately. Welfare-to-work programmes in Britain do not really exist to get the unemployed back into employment. Instead, they exist to legitimate a particular form of labour market organisation (that is, highly flexible), upon which a wider model for economic growth rests. Accordingly, Britain's low expenditure on labour market programmes can be explained by the fact that it concentrates spending almost exclusively on job-search services, and commits virtually nothing to occupational training.

The Work Programme's real priority is to reinforce the desirability and necessity of certain behaviours at the individual level. Participants must be ready for any job. Its target audience is not those out of work – because the superficial nature of interventions would be unable to address the structural barriers to work that most people face – but rather those *in work*, who are effectively intimidated into tempering their expectations of reward and decent treatment. The argument that the Work Programme is failing young people rests therefore on the assumption that the state is actually trying to help, just getting it badly wrong – in practice there can be no such comfort.[13]

The Work Programme has to be seen in the more general context of the conditionality agenda around benefits provision. Mandatory work activity for JSA recipients, even before they enter the Work Programme, led to the notorious case of Cait Reilly, who sued the government for forcing her to take an unpaid placement in Poundland, instead of a voluntary position in a museum more suited to her educational background and ambitions.[14] The case exposed the absurdity of welfare-to-work for today's young people. But it also exposed its central purpose: in neoliberal logic, Britain has far too many over-skilled university-leavers willing and able to work in museums, funded by an over-stretched public sector, but far too few people willing to work in the growth industry of discount retail.

A new political economy of work

The overriding aim of labour market policy is to establish employment – irrespective of pay and quality – as the only important contribution an individual can make to society. Those who expect to enjoy the benefits and protections of twenty-first-century Britain must contribute in this way. Unemployment is therefore seen through a highly individualised lens, rather than conceived as a collective problem to be addressed at the macroeconomic level.

Is there scope to re-collectivise unemployment? American economist L. Randall Wray has advocated a job guarantee programme whereby the state becomes the 'employer of last resort', offering community-centred employment opportunities for any citizen, at any time. Unemployment would be consigned to history, and it would also drive up pay and conditions among private sector employers as they would be compelled to beat those available in the scheme.[15]

Although the idea instinctively feels progressive, Wray overlooks the long history of subsidised or 'sheltered' employment in Europe. French-speaking countries typically use public sector employment to maintain the skills of those made unemployed in declining industries. In the UK, subsidised public or third sector employment was part of the New Labour government's New Deal for Young People (up to 2007) and the Future Jobs Fund (from 2008), and the coalition government until recently offered something similar for young people through Youth Contracts. Although Wray's scheme would be organised on a much larger scale, he fails to address the stigmatisation that invariably results from participation in such schemes, and the inconvenient truth that a steady supply of immigrant workers, who would not be entitled to participate, willing to accept low pay and poor conditions undermines any compulsion for the private sector to match what is on offer in the public sector.

It also ignores the reality of the type of jobs economies like Britain now create: low-skilled, services sector jobs. If a job-guarantee scheme were preparing young people for the private sector, there is a danger of merely replicating this business model using taxpayer funds. The only comprehensive way to improve young people's experience of employment is to transform British financial and industrial policy. The financial sector must be refocused on long-term investment in productive activity which generates high-quality jobs. And corporate governance should be reformed so that companies replace the short-termist focus on maximising their share price, with the long-term pursuit of socially useful business activity.

Yet a great deal can be done even within the narrower confines of labour market policy. A higher minimum wage, aggressively enforced, would be a start. Zero hours contracts (and similar arrangements where only a small number of hours are guaranteed) can and must be outlawed. We need a sea-change in apprenticeship provision, so that employers are legally compelled to offer meaningful opportunities to people leaving education. Moreover, we need a benefits system that rewards rather than punishes young people for trying to combine work and education, facilitating rather than problematising transitions to adulthood.

There remains the enormous question, however, of how we get from here to there. How should young people mobilise? In short, we need a new political economy that actually challenges the way work is organised in the economy in general, with radical trade unionism at its heart. It is easy to imagine that trade unions have abandoned today's young people, that they are more interested in protecting the perks of their existing, older members, concentrated in the public sector, than in mobilising among young people in new private sector workplaces. However, taking this view would mean swallowing the neoliberal demonisation of trade unionism, a discourse which seems to have infected even the Labour Party leadership.

It would also mean ignoring the Thatcherite reforms which cornered trade unions into the public sector, and the tireless work that many unions do to try to expand their reach. The campaign for inter-generational justice has been far too eager to criticise trade unions for defending their members' pension arrangements (which have been viciously attacked in recent years), in the process reinforcing the sense that trade unions represent 'vested interests'. This is exactly what the neoliberal elite wants us to believe.

This is not to say that tried and tested ways of organising are all that are required. Does relying on traditional trade union organisation make sense when so few of us make a living from a 'trade', and employers' profits are less dependent on vocational skills? It is not at all surprising that young people are less willing to join a trade union when they have no idea how many hours they will be working this week, and whether they will have a job at all next week. And trade unions work best when the majority of the members of a workplace are members, enabling collective negotiation.

There is no doubt that a historic realignment needs to take place, to make trade unionism more relevant to how work is experienced by young people today. This means organising among the unemployed and the precariously employed, and trade unions offering the kind of support to young people that the neoliberal state refuses to provide.

But this requires young people themselves to mobilise – embracing trade unionism in order to renew it. If employers no longer fear strikes because low-skilled workers are interchangeable, then we need to take industrial unrest into new areas, such as collective refusal to participate in mandatory work activity and the Work Programme. These policies will quickly crumble when private providers are no longer getting paid due to a lack of clients, or when Job Centre Plus is faced with the prospect of sanctioning all or most of their recipients at the same time.

Consumption strikes also need to take on a new prominence; if we cannot hurt the worst employers through withholding labour, we can dent their revenue by refusing to buy their goods and services, or those of the companies they supply. This will not just send a message to the individual companies boycotted, but undermine Britain's flawed economic model. Young people are the victims of this model, but also in some ways its perpetrators, in their willingness to consume (invariably accruing debt in order to do so). Trade unions have the natural advantage to organise resistance – but young people must set the tone.

Dr Craig Berry is Deputy Director at the Sheffield Political Economy Research Institute at the University of Sheffield. His previous roles include Pensions Policy Officer at the TUC, Policy Advisor at HM Treasury, and Head of Policy at the International Longevity Centre. His book *Globalisation and Ideology in Britain: Neoliberalism, Free Trade and the Global Economy* was published by Manchester University Press in 2011.

Notes

1. George Osborne, 'Chancellor speaks on tax and benefits', speech delivered on 31 March 2014, available at https://www.gov.uk/government/speeches/chancellor-speaks-on-tax-and-benefits.
2. Gill Valentine, 'Inequality and class prejudice in an age of austerity', SPERI British Political Economy Brief No.8, 2014, available at http://

speri.dept.shef.ac.uk/wp-content/uploads/2014/10/Brief8-inequality-and-class-prejudice-in-an-age-of-austerity.pdf.

3. Craig Berry, 'The final nail in the coffin? Crisis, manufacturing decline, and why it matters', in Jeremy Green, Colin Hay and Peter Taylor-Gooby (eds), *The British Growth Crisis: The Search for a New Model*, Palgrave, 2015, pp 174-200.

4. Anne Wren, 'The political economy of the service transition', *Renewal: A Journal of Social Democracy* 21(1), 2013, available at http://www.renewal.org.uk/articles/the-political-economy-of-the-service-transition.

5. Craig Berry, 'The hyper-Anglicisation of active labour market policy: facilitating and exemplifying a flawed growth model', SPERI Paper No.14, 2014, available at http://speri.dept.shef.ac.uk/wp-content/uploads/2014/06/SPERI-Paper-No.-14.pdf; Colin Hay, *The Failure of Anglo-Liberal Capitalism*, Palgrave, 2013.

6. Maria Hudson, Casualisation and Low Pay, Trades Union Congress, 2014, available at http://www.tuc.org.uk/sites/default/files/Casualisationandlowpay.docx.

7. Richard Murphy, *Disappearing Fast: The Falling Income of the UK's Self-Employed People*, Tax Research LLP, 2013, available at http://www.taxresearch.org.uk/Documents/SEI2013.pdf.

8. Paul Sissons and Katy Jones, *Lost in Translation? The Changing Labour Market and Young People Not in Education, Employment or Training*, The Work Foundation.

9. Office for National Statistics, Labour Market Statistics: February 2015, available at http://www.ons.gov.uk/ons/publications/re-reference-tables.html?edition=tcm%3A77-350752.

10. Jonny Wright & Paul Sissons, *The Skills Dilemma: Skills Under-Utilisation and Low-Wage Work*, The Work Foundation, 2012, available at http://www.theworkfoundation.com/DownloadPublication/Report/307_Skills%20Dilemma.pdf.

11. Kevin Rawlinson, 'Work programme creates just 48,000 long-term jobs in three years', *The Guardian*, 21 March 2014, available at http://www.theguardian.com/society/2014/mar/21/work-programme-creates-48000-long-term-jobs-three-years.

12. Craig Berry, 'Quantity over quality: a political economy of "active labour market policy" in the UK', *Policy Studies* 35(6), 2014, pp 592-610.

13. *Ibid.*

14. BBC News, 'Back-to-work scheme breached laws, says Court of Appeal', 12 February 2013, available at http://www.bbc.co.uk/news/business-21426928.

15. L. Randall Wray, 'The job guarantee: a government plan for full employment', *The Nation*, 27 June 2011, available at http://www.thenation.com/article/161249/job-guarantee-government-plan-full-employment#.

Plan F and the care crisis: why we need feminist economics

Polly Trenow

We've been taught that if we work hard, we will be rewarded with wealth. Our success, or lack of it, is up to us; our lives are what we make of them.

Yet for most people, this apparent choice is an illusion. The single biggest indicator for poverty in later life is to be born into poverty. The structural barriers that keep the poor poor are not only already firmly in place, but they have also been reinforced by the coalition government's austerity policies.

Increasingly, women are told that childbearing is also a choice. Cultural norms mean that women take on the burden of caring for children, as well as for elderly and disabled relatives. 57 per cent of unpaid carers are women, and unpaid care work can be detrimental both to economic prospects and to health.[1] In the last estimate, the value of unpaid care work was £119 billion.[2] But in an economy where success is measured only by monetary profit, there is no room to give unpaid care work this value.

The stagnation of wages, and changes in working patterns, mean that more women than ever are in paid work. The unpaid care work that these women used to do, is now taken on by other, less well-off women in a paid capacity: 80 per cent of paid care workers are women.[3]

Carers play a pivotal role in society, doing a job for little or no pay, doing work which would otherwise cost the government billions. And most carers do so to the detriment of their future prosperity.

Children, old age and sickness are inevitable; care is not an individual choice. Unfortunately, decades of neoliberal capitalism have worn away the idea of collective responsibility. This prevents us from acknowledging that the government, businesses and the public have a duty of care.

The care crisis

The coalition government boasts that there are 'more women in the workforce than ever before', 14.1 million to be exact.[4] If this is the case, who is doing the care work?

The commercialisation of care has opened up paid employment in roles that used be unpaid. In England, 11 per cent of those aged 80 and over receive institutional care in residential and nursing care homes. 80 per cent of all care workers are women, 17 per cent are Black, Asian and Minority Ethnic (BAME), and 19 per cent are migrants.[5] In London more than 60 per cent of all care workers are born outside of the UK.[6] Migrant women who come to the UK in search of safety or economic prosperity can find themselves trapped in this low-paid, insecure work. They also frequently report exploitation. Their work is not only devalued because it is 'women's work', but also increasingly because it is the work of women of colour.

Women like Offir feel the care crisis strongly.[7] Offir moved to the UK from Poland to earn more money. Despite having a Polish master's degree, she works in a care home because it is the only work she can find to fit in around her own caring responsibilities – for her four-year-old daughter and elderly father. She told me: 'The type of job I am doing is a must, because I have to survive ... I will wait until my daughter goes to school next year and then maybe I can change it'.

Like many single mothers, Offir feels she often has to choose between economic success and caring responsibilities. She doesn't like her job in the care home, she finds it boring, but it is still more secure than employment in Poland.

Men may be taking on more domestic responsibility, but this mostly happens where women work in professional and skilled jobs.[8] For working-class women, the care and domestic work gender split has changed little over the last few decades.[9] Recently, childcare costs have rocketed, now costing around £7500 a year.[10] This penalises poorer families: if the lower paid worker in a household – usually female – doesn't earn enough to cover childcare, she may be forced back into the home. As Offir said, 'I want to do more hours but the nursery is so expensive I'm not sure I can afford it'.

Young carers under twenty-four are suffering the most from incremental deterioration of their general health as they provide more unpaid care. Those working full-time and providing fifty hours or more of unpaid care per week are up to three times more likely to report their health as 'not good' than those providing no unpaid care.[11] On top of this, inflexible work schedules make it difficult to combine care and work. Women like Offir face a lack of good quality, well-paid jobs that both allow them to work at their skill level and are flexible enough to fit around their caring responsibilities.

Austerity has also hit the pockets of women far harder than those of men, with 85 per cent of the reductions to tax and benefits coming from women's incomes.[12] This is especially true of women from BAME communities, who are more likely to be living in poverty in the first place and therefore more reliant on working benefits or tax credits.[13] The coalition government's cuts to public sector jobs, where women and particularly BAME women predominate, have forced thousands of women out of well-paid, secure jobs into low-paid private sector employment, often on temporary and minimum-hours contracts.[14] In addition, drastic reductions in public services like Sure Start Centres and public transport have made it increasingly difficult for carers to work alongside their caring responsibilities.[15]

These drastic cuts to social care and public sector jobs, combined with an ever-ageing population, record birth rates, and the intersecting oppressions of gender, race and class, have lead to this care crisis.

Why should young people care about the care crisis?

Few young activists are aware of the care crisis. Feminism may be popular right now, but the focus is too often on sexual harassment, body image or other indicators of inequality, which are given more airtime by the mainstream media. Maybe this is because feminism is dominated by white, childless, middle-class women for whom the burden of care is less pressing. While young women are certainly disillusioned with party politics – only 39 per cent voted in the 2010 election – the nation's care crisis also remains low on their list of concerns.

This may be because for many women the inequality of care does not reveal itself until they have children. The pay gap between men and women in their twenties is relatively small (5 per cent) compared to those in their forties (24 per cent). Even so, 14 per cent of young women cannot work because they have caring responsibilities. Their voices, like those of so many other groups of carers, are marginalised, too often tarred as 'scroungers'. So the voices of women whose economic prospects are most seriously dented by their care work (working-class women, women of colour and migrant women) are at the same time those voices most marginalised – both within mainstream media and by mainstream feminism.

Plan F: what would a feminist economy do to tackle these issues?

Plan F is a vision for an alternative feminist economy created by the Women's Budget Group.[16] A feminist economy would provide women and men with a real choice, in which caring for your loved ones does not permanently cripple your economic prospects. In this proposed economy, care is well supported and highly valued.

Too often, spending on social security is deemed a 'cost' with no recognition of the money that is saved in the long run, by supporting the most vulnerable in our society and their carers. Four year election terms for governments exacerbate this short-term thinking. We need to radically re-think.

Plan F would properly invest in state social care provision and support those who do it unpaid. It would revolutionise the labour market and, rather than pushing women into the boardroom, would democratise the workplace from the bottom up so the lowest paid (who are predominantly women) have a real say in their employment conditions. Trade unions are one part of this, but women's low representation in senior roles within unions, despite the fact that they make up the bulk of members, is something we should remain concerned about.

Plan F would raise the minimum wage to a living wage for all and would drastically improve the employment rights and working conditions of paid carers.

Flexible working is also part of Plan F, but a *feminist* definition of flexible working. The proponents of zero-hours and short-term contracts have argued that this provides flexibility. But when underemployment is rife and in-work poverty outstrips out-of-work poverty, it is clear this kind of flexible work is not the right approach.

Plan F would challenge gender norms in care by ensuring that men received paternity leave of at least a year, paid at their salary. This would extend to the other parent in same sex couples. All parental leave arrangements would also be applicable to couples who have children through surrogacy – an arrangement which is currently excluded from paid leave entitlements.

Plan F would match spending on physical infrastructure with equal investment in social infrastructure – education, health and care provision. This would, in the long term, provide more secure jobs for all genders, and also tackle the care crisis head on.

Our economy must be fairer for carers, but the fundamental shift should be in how we value care. Campaigns like Wages for Housework have existed since the 1970s, not calling simply for a sum of money, but for a shift in perspective and a revaluing of women's work.[17] More recently, Mothers at Home Matter have been calling for greater financial support to enable parents or other caregivers to stay at home and provide care.[18]

Unpaid care work has never been included in economic measures, most notably Gross Domestic Product (GDP). Yet this exhausting and important work has propped up our economy for hundreds of years. The Office of National Statistics has recently started to value unpaid work from households in the UK including childcare, adult care and voluntary work through their Household Satellite Account.[19] Perhaps when we understand the true impact of unpaid care work we may also see an improvement in how we value paid care work.

The government may be wringing their hands about the fiscal deficit, but for the Women's Budget Group it is the care deficit that is of most concern. Only when we see a feminist economy that divides the responsibility of care fairly, will we really tackle the care crisis – and begin to approach a solution to gender inequality.

Polly Trenow has been part of the Women's Budget Group (www.wbg. org.uk) since 2009 and is currently on the Management Committee. She has worked in women's rights and gender equality since 2005 and combines a passion for feminist economics and with working as a freelance educator in schools and educational institutions.

Notes

1. ONS Census data 2013 http://www.ons.gov.uk/ons/rel/census/2011-census/detailed-characteristics-for-local-authorities-in-england-and-wales/rpt---unpaid-care.html and 'Migrant Care Workers in Ageing Societies:

Research Findings in the United Kingdom', COMPAS, ESRC Centre on Migration, Policy and Society, 2010.

2. 'Valuing carers – calculating the value of carers' support', Carers UK, Circle and the University of Leeds, 2011. http://circle.leeds.ac.uk/files/2012/08/110512-circle-carers-uk-valuing-carers.pdf

3. 'Migrant Care Workers in Ageing Societies: Research Findings in the United Kingdom', COMPAS, ESRC Centre on Migration, Policy and Society, 2010.

4. Nigel Morris, 'More women are in work than ever before', *The Independent*, 23 October 2014. http://www.independent.co.uk/news/uk/politics/more-women-are-in-work-in-britain-than-ever-before-9811845.html

5. 'Migrant Care Workers in Ageing Societies: Research Findings in the United Kingdom', COMPAS, ESRC Centre on Migration, Policy and Society, 2010.

6. *Ibid.*

7. My own research, names have been changed.

8. A 14 and 15 per cent drop respectively in women saying that the bulk of domestic and care work falls solely to them. 'Great expectations: exploring the promises of gender equality', IPPR, 2013.

9. Women in partly skilled or unskilled jobs have only experienced a 7 per cent drop. 'Great expectations: exploring the promises of gender equality', IPPR 2013.

10. Annual Cost of Childcare Survey, Family and Childcare Trust, 2014. http://www.familyandchildcaretrust.org/childcare-costs-surveys

11. Census data from 2011.

12. Andrew Grice, 'Women bear 85 per cent of burden after coalition's tax and benefit tweaks', *The Independent*, 6 December 2014. http://www.independent.co.uk/news/uk/politics/women-bear-85-of-burden-after-coalitions-tax-and-benefit-tweaks-9907143.html

13. 'Layers of Inequality A Human Rights and Equality Impact Assessment of the Public Spending Cuts on Black Asian and Minority Ethnic Women in Coventry', 2013. http://www.barrowcadbury.org.uk/wp-content/uploads/2013/09/layers_of_inequality.pdf

14. 65 per cent of public sector workers are women, Unison, 2013. http://www.unison.org.uk/about/our-organisation/member-groups/women/key-issues/women-and-public-spending-cuts/home/

15. More than 600 Sure Start Centres have closed or merged since 2010 according to analysis from the Labour Party, Oliver Wright, 'Sure Start centres risk closure, says Labour', *The Independent*, 10 August 2014. http://www.independent.co.uk/news/uk/politics/sure-start-centres-risk-closure-says-labour-9659503.html

16. Women's Budget Group http://wbg.org.uk

17. Dayna Tortorici, 'More Smiles, More Money', N+1, Issue 17, Autumn 2013. https://nplusonemag.com/issue-17/reviews/more-smiles-more-money/

18. http://www.mothersathomematter.co.uk/
19. 'Household Satellite Account (HHSA) (experimental)', Office for National Statistics. http://www.ons.gov.uk/ons/guide-method/method-quality/specific/social-and-welfare-methodology/household-satellite-account/index.html

Communities of defence: legal political organising after the riots

Wail Qasim

Political organising is more and more a necessity. It is a collective labour undertaken to both protect ourselves and to make political gains. If 'politics is the continuation of war by other means',[1] then political organising is the strategy and tactics of this war. It may be the case that liberal democracies tend not to collapse entirely into civil war, but they are the stage on which major political eruptions and uprisings take place with increasing regularity.

Rioting is, at least at its surface, the most war-like challenge to the state and its political orthodoxy that can be enacted from within the state itself. Within the space of ten key months from November 2010 to August 2011 Britain saw three major riotous acts: the student protests of late 2010; the collective destruction of private property in the West End of London on the 26 March 'March for the Alternative' and uprisings across England after the killing of Mark Duggan in August 2011.

The above examples share many similarities but it would be wrong to collapse them into one another. A sensitive, successful reckoning with just one would be difficult enough. I want to avoid creating a false genealogy in which each of these events would be seen as leading to the next. Rather, these major riotous acts might be seen as a constellation from which a complex web of smaller and more fleeting political expressions emerged.

I want to look at how different organisers and communities have continued the 'war' by other means, in particular, in the resistance to the 2014 killing of Michael Brown in Ferguson in the United States. The scale of these current riotous acts also presents a greater opportunity for collective organising than has been seen for some time. It is important, therefore, to look back at what happened after the eruptions of 2011. What was the state's reaction? What practices were developed to resist that reaction?

There are two major types of response to the legal ramifications of riotous actions: left activist legal resistance and community legal resistance. Both of these have separately developed techniques and practices necessary to effectively respond to criminalisation and brutalisation. Despite recent positive moves towards establishing a dialogue between these two modes of organising, there is still a common political project to foster. Both share a common enemy in the law: the law is totalising, after all. Combating stop and search on Brixton high street is just as important as monitoring stop and search on large demonstrations. Developing a politics of collective resistance to the law in everyday life seems like the logical next step for radical organising.

Reckoning with 2011

From the riotous acts of 2011 to the resistance of today, the longest-lasting scars have not been the damage inflicted to buildings but the wounds inflicted by police, courts and prisons. The aftermath of each of these moments was a story of people and their communities pitted against the law: implemented as the state's biggest weapon. During the riotous act the law is on the back foot; it is as if there is no law. And so often the law later reclaims lost ground with brute force. This was made clear in the arrest and accelerated processing of thousands of people, through all-night court sessions during the August 2011 riots.

While being prosecuted renders the defendant powerless, for a long time activists and organisers have fought back against the political victimisation of individuals. The Industrial Workers of the World slogan, 'an injury to one is an injury to all' has been the principal motivation behind much political organising. This phrase was something of an internal motto for Defend The Right To Protest (DtRtP), a campaign set up in response to the large arrests during the 2010 student demonstrations. DtRtP serves as only one example of how politically organised leftists seek to defend those targeted and criminalised for their political resistance.

I have been a part of left legal support organisations since 2011, and have campaigned with DtRtP on the criminalisation of students and others. Yet the distance between this type of work and community legal resistance has led me to ask the question: what about those who resist oppression in ways not conventionally seen as 'political'? The 2011 riots clearly had political causes yet were almost universally deemed illegitimate as a political act. Though the riots were on a much larger scale, the police response and subsequent prosecutions were similar to what anti-cuts protesters faced earlier in the year and our legal support organisations were active in the latter. Why then were they absent from the twenty-four hour courts? What was it that removed us from the communities dealing with the aftermath of the riots?

By the time of the summer of the riots, many of us had become used to sitting through court hearings in support of those prosecuted. We had begun to develop a system of legal support that was both radical and worked alongside standard legal representation. This piece asks why we were not there in August 2011 and aims to compel our presence the next time such a grand blow is dealt by the state.

The first half of 2011

250 people were arrested as part of (the infantilisingly titled) Operation Malone,[2] in a huge operation designed to quickly make examples out of some of those who participated in that first major bout of unrest during the Conservative-led coalition government. Malone was a 'criminal investigation following the commission of offences during a number of demonstrations against the raising of university tuition fees'.[3] A huge number of young people who had demonstrated against students being priced out of higher education found themselves charged with 'violent disorder'. 'Violent disorder' is a criminal offence under Section 2 of the Public Order Act of 1986. It is second in severity only to 'riot', a charge rarely used, making it one of the most serious public order offences in English law. Those charged with violent disorder face up to five years in prison.

Facing trial is a stressful and damaging experience, even where the charge is relatively minimal. Here, over 100 people not only faced the long drawn out punishment of the criminal justice system itself, but also the possibility of imprisonment for lengthy periods of time. Edward Woollard, who threw a fire extinguisher from the roof of Conservative party headquarters Millbank Tower, was sentenced to two years and eight months in prison. Charlie Gilmour found himself sentenced to sixteen months in prison after swinging from a flag attached to the cenotaph. Both pled guilty to their charges, yet were still met with heavy sentences. The prospect of these sentences also weighed heavily on those who pled not guilty and instead waited on verdicts months and years away.

In response to the large number of arrests and charges, left-wing legal support groups began to organise in defence of those criminalised. The Legal Defence and Monitoring Group (LDMG) and the then newly formed Green and Black Cross (GBC) both provided legal observers to monitor police during the demonstrations, made sure arrestees were met as they were released from police stations and would later sit through defendants' trials. Defend the Right to Protest was also founded at this time and took on the political element of the legal defence, campaigning around the political nature of the prosecutions, which was most evident in the blanket use of the violent disorder charge. Many of these techniques of activist legal defence are longstanding, having previously been employed in similar circumstances, but many of those learning how to undertake the work were new to this kind of campaigning. This massive state legal attack would also prompt the formalisation of previously *ad hoc* support. We put structures in place to respond when the next attack arrived, as it inevitably would.

It came on 26 March 2011. Protests around the TUC 'March for the Alternative' demonstration led to 149 UK Uncut protesters being arrested for a sit-in at the Piccadilly luxury store Fortnum and Mason. The police also arrested other protesters employing the 'Black Bloc' tactic of collective anonymity to inflict property damage around the West End of London. A portion of those arrested on the UK Uncut protest were later charged with 'aggravated trespass', while others again faced the newly favoured 'violent disorder' charge.

Yet by this point an activist community had developed out of the student defence campaigns. We trained many more legal observers and we were present on the 26 March demonstration. From our presence at court hearings, it became obvious that courts picked on those who were alone, seeking to alienate them from their peers. The large turnout in the public galleries of these courts was both a shock and a nuisance to the judiciary.

Being present and bearing witness in courts as so-called justice took place, not only bore out methods of resistance for fighting the law by undermining its ability to isolate and individually punish (even prior to a verdict), but also begun to foster bigger conversations around what justice is and should be. Watching friends, comrades and even strangers go from arrest to bail to court to prison destroyed any semblance of agreement with this punishment system for many of those who were a part of the legal aftermath of the protests. The means-end implementation of the law had been laid out plainly in the state's nakedly political policing and prosecution. We were left with an unavoidable imperative to fight the law in its own courtrooms, as well as in the streets.

The second half of 2011

The killing of Mark Duggan in Tottenham led to a backlash with a force rarely seen. Riots lasted for several days across England with some, including then-Conservative MEP Roger Helmer (now of UKIP), calling for military force to quell disorder. That the army did not take to the streets doesn't, however, mean that the war was averted. It was continued by other means. Thousands were arrested, ending up in court. Nearly 2000 people were found guilty of offences related to the riots.[4] Again, a large proportion of those arrested were charged with violent disorder. But this time sentences were even harsher than those handed out earlier in the year.

Left-leaning people of various stripes were happy to support anger at the killing of Mark Duggan but when presented with scenes of looting, they called into question what they saw as 'consumerism' taken to its logical conclusion. Rioters attacking commercial spaces rather than police stations (though this also did happen) fed into a state-driven narrative in which riotous acts were rewritten as self-interested and apolitical. Those levelling this critique had forgotten, or refused to acknowledge, that people have to consume in order to reproduce their lives. Consumption of useful items isn't what is wrong with capitalism; placing these goods for sale with no regard to people's needs is. This short-sighted condemnation of looting stems from a position of privilege. Only those sure of their own security under capitalism could make such a claim. This exemplifies the way in which, for many people on the left, the political nature of an act is both narrowly defined and premised on class and race privilege.

The political content of the riots may well have come in an unfamiliar form, but the repressive response was the familiar succession of brutal policing, media demonisation and carceral example-making. These repressive tactics stand in a direct relationship to those of earlier in the year.

During the near suspension of 'public order' a collective resistance emerged. In response, the state targeted the collectivity, alienating and isolating individuals by trafficking them swiftly from street to prison in a matter of hours. Many did not even have access to legal representation. It was here that the absence of left legal activists was most felt. Organisations like LDMG, GBC and DtRtP did not have nearly enough resources to intervene *en masse*, but what little response there was from the activist left was individual and *ad hoc*.

An organised collective response may not have been easy, but it certainly was necessary. The reasons for its lack should be explained (without falling into providing excuses) in order to learn from the mistakes made. There is no good reason why techniques developed within activist circles should not have been used during the riots, particularly as left critiques of society typically lead away from such NIMBY politics towards universal struggle. More recently, groups like DtRtP have moved toward linking up, for example, death in custody campaigns with their protest work. A radical transformatory politics should lead to community legal defence and resistance being applied wherever the law oppresses, this failure to react can be explained by looking at differentially applied conceptions of political community.

Political organising seems to happen within communities, but the specific nature of the community in question appears to dictate the left response. Those brutalised or criminalised on an official anti-fascist demonstration are to be defended, they are part of the activist community, but it would seem beyond the scope of most organisations to defend someone who gets into an individual fight with a person expressing fascist or racist views. But it is more in line with a radical approach to organising to base the scope of the community one seeks to defend not on the context of their actions but rather on the commonality of the oppressive repression they face. When the application of the law is already biased in favour of those who typically are party to greater defence and support, can we afford to be choosey about who stands within the defended community?

The reality is that it fell on the shoulders of 'communities' to defend their own after the riots were over. In some places, like Tottenham, there is a long history of organising not only in response to police killings but also in defence of those who take part in the uprisings that follow them. Family members, friends and neighbours stepped up where they could. Community defence meetings took places in Tottenham and Hackney. Residents and local organisers established 'Stop Criminalising Hackney Youth'. Unfortunately, by this point the criminalisation had already happened: many were already counting down the days until the end of their prison sentences.

Community legal organising

My aim is not to galvanise a new community. Nor do I want a new communitarian politics. The space for communality that I refer to is already in existence, but needs careful highlighting to bring it to the fore. By expanding the terrain on which we deploy the technics of legal support that have developed over the last few years, we can begin to bring the legitimacy of the law into question. The burgeoning #BlackLivesMatter and 'I can't breathe' movement sparked by the killing of Michael Brown in Ferguson, Missouri, is exactly an opportunity for putting this into practice. An organisation like DtRtP, that began as a defence campaign for criminalised students, has already begun to form the links necessary for such a response by working to support the campaigns of families who have suffered the loss of a loved one at the hands of the state. Most recently DtRtP along with NUS Black Students and other organisations brought Ferguson activists to the UK to speak to students, activists and communities.

The wealth of protest action across the United States has taken the form of civil disobedience, and direct action against the state and its ability to administrate life smoothly. We are yet to see such a move this side of the Atlantic, but the potential is there. In the latter part of 2014 The London Black Revolutionaries began to import some of the 'shut it down' tactics seen in the US, closing roads and shopping centres, taking to Westfield shopping centre in White City for the second of two London-to-Ferguson solidarity actions. The #BlackLivesMatter movement has in part been so successful because of its vitalist strain. Unlike traditional left meta-narratives about oppression, this movement's orientation toward life has rooted it firmly in concerns of everyday repression. This rhetoric has clearly rung true with many people, drawing huge crowds to protests globally. While many of the campaigners at the heart of the movement would describe themselves as 'anti-capitalists', they don't fall into the trap of patronising black crowds by telling them that their concerns stem from prevailing economic conditions. They already know this. Instead the movement demands that we take black life seriously and does so by questioning our fundamental relationship to the state and law. In fact, this movement posits black life as in opposition to (and free of) the state and law.

Everyday legal defence is a necessity if we are to organise with life as a central category for our politics. Some of this work is already being done by community groups, new and old. Newham Monitoring Project (NMP), for example, tackles stop and search and arrests within its borough and surrounding areas, putting into practice the partly forgotten principle of 'don't walk on by' that was widely practiced against the sus laws – a precursor to modern stop and search legislation – in areas such as Brixton in the 1980s and 1990s. In taking on this day-to-day casework, this relatively small monitoring project poses a credible threat to the police's ability to harass and discriminate. Recent revelations that the NMP were subject to undercover police surveillance only serve to highlight this.[5]

The London Campaign Against Police and State Violence (LCAPSV) is an example of a very young organisation that has set itself the vast task of community defence. LCAPSV take on casework that seeks to challenge everything from minor charges of 'obstructing a constable',[6] to the police's notoriously dangerous and deadly 'hard stop' (where firearms police use their vehicles to bring a suspect's car to an abrupt stop. This manoeuvre was deployed in the killings of Mark Duggan and Azelle Rodney). Like the US proponents of the #BlackLivesMatter movement, LCAPSV's value lies in its ability to trace the thread that runs from the law in the abstract to police and state violence as it is meted out daily on the streets.

Part of the answer is that more people on the left – and it is particularly white activists who should heed this call – need to see this kind of community casework as vital political organising. The ruthless critique of society proposed by most strands of left thought should lead us to the conclusion that all policing is political. All prisoners are political prisoners. If we are to see a radical transformation of society and an end to state violence we have to start from everyday street-level community legal support. This kind of work directly leads to the kind of support necessary in the aftermath of mass tumultuous actions.

Another riotous eruption will not be far off: let's prepare ourselves now.

Wail Qasim is an activist campaigning with Defend the Right to Protest and other groups working on community justice, anti-racism and anti-fascism. He also writes and has contributed work to *The Guardian* and *The Independent* amongst other places. His blog can be found at: isthisday.com

Notes

1. Michel Foucault, *Society Must Be Defended*, London, 2004, p. 15.
2. Freedom of information request, Metropolitan Police, as at 16 March 2012. http://www.met.police.uk/foi/pdfs/disclosure_2012/march_2012/2012030000380.pdf
3. Freedom of information request, Metropolitan Police. http://www.met.police.uk/foi/pdfs/disclosure_2012/may_2012/2012040002310.pdf
4. Simon Rogers, 'Riots broken down: who was in court and what's happened to them?' *The Guardian*, 4 July 2012. http://www.theguardian.com/news/datablog/2012/jul/04/riot-defendants-court-sentencing
5. Rob Evans and Pail Lewis, 'Scotland Yard spied on critics of police corruption', *The Guardian*, 24 June 2013. http://www.theguardian.com/uk/2013/jun/24/metropolitan-police-spying-undercover-officers
6. Police in the context of a stop and search often deploy this charge where no other reason to criminalise is found. The subject of the arrest is said to have obstructed the fruitless search thus creating a crime where one previously didn't exist.

Co-operatives: resisting the housing crisis

Mike Shaw and Sean Farmelo

The British economy is fundamentally tied in with the state of housing. An intentionally limited supply of houses, alongside government subsidies for homeowners and landlords, has inflated house prices at a staggering rate since the 1970s. If the price of food had increased at the same rate as house prices, then a standard supermarket chicken would now cost over £50.[1]

The majority of wealth held by individuals in the UK is now in housing: more than twice that of pensions and life insurance, and five times that held in shares, bonds and other securities.[2] But it is far from evenly spread. The 2 per cent of Britons who are landlords have seen their housing wealth more than double in the past decade, to over £800 billion.[3]

This chapter will explore the nature and history of Britain's housing crisis; the privatisation of the public housing stock in the 1980s; the subsequent failure of the market to provide sufficient, suitable or affordable housing; and the systemic impact that this is having on young people and wider society. We will discuss potential solutions to the housing crisis, the history of housing struggles, and finally alternative, collective models of housing provision, with a particular focus on the setting up of the Edinburgh Student Housing Co-operative.

The state of housing

The upper classes benefit from the housing crisis through their disproportionate ownership – becoming further enriched by increases in house prices. With wealth comes power, and so it is that successive government policies have served to further inflate house prices at the expense of the rest of us. Speculators sit on land, waiting for prices to rise rather than building much-needed homes. Developers pressure local councils to grant inappropriate planning permissions for unaffordable, sub-standard housing, against the will of local communities.[4] Through numerous means, investors, developers and landlords – with the help of the state – are able to reshape and restyle entire neighbourhoods and cities, and in doing so, reshape society at large. This is ultimately all in the interest of maximising profits: tenants are reliant on a place to live, while landlords benefit from their surplus property.

As house prices continue to inflate, the divide between those who do, and those who do not, outright own their homes increases. Students in England are now graduating with an average of £44,000 debt, supposedly to confer a job-market advantage against their non-student peers.[5] We are a generation with poor prospects, burdened in debt, competing against one another for a limited supply of underpaid, unsatisfying jobs. Yet in the decade leading up to 2003 the richest tenth of families saw their housing wealth increase by £61,842 to £82,490 per child. The state of housing is further entrenching class divide: Britain now has arguably the worst levels of social mobility in the Western world.[6]

Housing wealth is also grossly distorted geographically, with location being the key decider of a house's value within the market. Nationally, London's housing stock is equivalent in market value to all of the housing in the next forty biggest British cities and towns combined.[7] Meanwhile, chronic disinvestment within many working class neighbourhoods has created prime opportunities for developers to profit. London is the most extreme example of this: working class tenants are being evicted and priced ever further out of the city.

The flipside of home ownership is housing debt. Many of those with mortgages simply cannot afford them, while others go into debt just to cover the rent. The possible need to work more to pay off mortgages or rent arrears reduces time available for family life, helping out in the local community, or organising for social and political change.

Around 290,000 new homes need to be built in England each year to meet growing demand.[8] The current rate of building is not even half that, and shows no signs of increasing.[9] This situation is not accidental, the product of poor planning or government incompetence – quite the contrary. It is the direct and explicit result of over three decades of intentional government policy. A limited supply of housing drives up property prices. Other policies, such as opting not to build social housing in wealthier areas, serve the same purpose. The low interest rates encouraged by the Treasury under both New Labour and the Coalition has encouraged more people to take on mortgages. This mean there is yet more competition in the housing market – further driving up house prices and drawing more people into debt.[10] Those already rich in housing wealth – who are not saddled in debt – see their properties rise further in value. The net subsidy enjoyed by homeowners, through schemes such as capital gains tax, amounts to over £12 billion a year. Landlords benefit from around £13 billion a year in tax reliefs.[11]

In 1980, newly elected Prime Minister Margaret Thatcher began the biggest privatisation in British history: 'Right to Buy'. This policy allowed council housing tenants to purchase their homes at heavily discounted prices. Advocates argued that it gave working class tenants a leg up onto the property ladder, enacting the Thatcherite vision of a so-called 'property-owning democracy'. The government specifically prevented councils from spending the money on building new houses to replace the ones they had sold. Over £40 billion of housing stock – two million homes – has been sold off and lost to the private sector.[12] Much of this is no longer in the hands of working class families; for example in London, 36 per cent of former council housing is now let out by private landlords.[13]

In the 1980s, the Thatcher government also significantly removed tenant rights, making it easier for landlords to take possession from renters,[14] driving up profitability for the private rental sector at the expense of tenants. Landlords were permitted, therefore, to more easily discriminate against 'undesirable' tenants. Much of this was absorbed through greater tenant dependency on housing benefit – effectively directly subsidising landlords. As one landlord put it himself:

> As a private landlord, I often think it is very telling that 80 per cent of my portfolio, purchased on the open market, were once bought under right to buy. So since over the years I have been paid LHA [Local Housing Allowance] per property totalling more than the council probably sold them for, you have to conclude right to buy is a crazy policy. The way it needs to work is for every unit sold, the funds are put in to building a new unit. Otherwise all you are doing is transferring social properties to private sector. It's great for people like me, but being honest not what I'd recommend a government do.[15]

From the end of the Second World War until Thatcher came into power, social housing was built at a rate in excess of 100,000 homes a year. She quartered that rate, and under successive governments it continued to decline.[16] In 2013-14, fewer than 10,000 new houses were built in the public sector. In two thirds of the country, effectively no social housing is being built at all.[17] There are over 1.8 million households, or 4.5 million people, on council housing waiting lists. In some London boroughs this accounts for a quarter of the population.[18] The lack of investment in new housing means that, incredibly, since 2008 the UK Treasury has been directly profiting from council housing.[19] These profits are then used to subsidise landlords and further inflate house prices.

As with so many of the privatisations by the Coalition and previous governments, the state retreats from providing basic services so that other providers are left to haphazardly fill the gap. The rhetoric of encouraging competition, cutting state bureaucracy and providing people with choice is used to dress up and cover up the lives being ruined. Other public services are contracted to private providers, allowing them to grossly profit from the state. In this case, state-provided social housing has been axed, with housing associations left to paper over the cracks – whilst more people are forced onto the private rental market, again pushing up the rents and maximising landlord profits.

Housing associations are not-for-profit charitable bodies providing social and affordable housing. They often manage former council housing stock and subsidise their charitable activities through for-profit housing. In outsourcing services, the state can also outsource responsibility for social housing provision, and in doing so can outsource blame for underfunding, poor provision and lack of supply.

The failure, or, depending on your perspective – success – of such policies can be seen every night in the doorways, underpasses and on the pavements of our cities. In the two years prior to 2013, rough sleeping increased by 60 per cent. On top of this, 'hidden' homelessness, including concealed tenants, sharing and overcrowding, affects 12 per cent of all households. Experience of homelessness is highest amongst urban, poor, young, black renters, who are lone parents or single.[20]

It can be tempting to blame homelessness on the immediate cause, whether it be benefit sanctions, job loss, domestic abuse, or any other of the myriad of ways people find themselves stuck without a home. Similarly, one can focus on tales of specific, exploitative landlords like the Jaguar-driving millionaire and aptly named thug Mark Fortune, who in 2013 was banned from being a landlord in Edinburgh after threatening to shoot tenants over a dispute over a maintenance bill.[21] But ultimately, such cases are all symptoms of a far deeper illness within society – a wider, systemic and unjustifiable failure to provide for one another when we are most in need. This failure is caused by the private market in housing. It is driven by profit.

Red Clydeside

The history of tenants' rights and housing reform is built on the extraordinary struggles of ordinary people. Only through such struggles has substantive change been achieved. Histories like these are generally little known, but struggles over housing have played key roles within wider class, race and gender struggles – ultimately playing a significant role in shaping our societies. A key example took place in Glasgow during the First World War, a struggle now known as Red Clydeside.[22]

In the early 1900s, nine tenths of the population rented from private landlords. Tenants had very few rights, and often lived in overcrowded and squalid housing. When the War began, a significant proportion of Glasgow's working-age men were away in the trenches, whilst many others were moving into the already overcrowded parts of the city to fulfil the need for more munitions workers. The city had faced years of growth, but little house building. Masters of opportunity, and viewing the women left behind as helpless, the city's landlords began to further exploit the situation to squeeze out profits. They began upping the rents and forcing evictions on those unable to pay, along with the growing numbers who simply refused to pay on principle.

Prior to the war, events such as the 11,000 strong Singer sewing machine strike in 1911, led by women workers, served to radicalise many in the city.[23] Groups such as the Co-operative Women's Guild provided spaces where women were empowered to become self-educated and partake in politics. One such woman was Mary Barbour, whose name has become synonymous with the subsequent struggle.[24]

Radicals among the urban poor began organising campaigning groups like the Glasgow Women's Housing Association. Women were stationed at key points in neighbourhoods on the lookout for the sheriffs officers, who were tasked with serving eviction notices, and the bailiffs. When spotted they would ring bells, sound whistles, and call out to their neighbours for assistance. Entire neighbourhoods would mobilise, filling the streets and blocking wynds,[25] entrances and doorways – making the officers' jobs impossible. People would mock the landlords and officers, branding them as unpatriotic – many of those facing eviction had family members at war. The movement developed strong ties with the local trade unions, who began threatening strike action, despite such action being outlawed during the war. The movement began to spread to other sites, and culminated in thousands marching through central Glasgow on 17 November 1915, ending in a standoff outside the Sheriff's Court.[26]

The unrest disturbed the government to such an extent that within five weeks they passed and began implementing the Increase of Rent and Mortgage Interest (War Restrictions) Act 1915 – fixing rents at their August 1914 level.

This period of Glasgow's history became known as Red Clydeside. Subsequent movements succeeded in winning the argument for rent controls right up until 1989.[27] For over seventy years the government actively regulated and restricted the amounts landlords were allowed to charge, significantly empowering and bettering the lives of tenants. Red Clydeside also bolstered and fuelled the drive for municipal housing – housing provided by the local authority at affordable rates, prioritising those most in need.

There are many more remarkable and influential examples of direct action by tenants throughout history, organising not only in their own interests, but in the interests of their communities through tactics such as rent strikes, resistance to evictions, protests and squatting. Across different contexts and cultures, such tactics have been used successfully time and again. From the 50,000 strong 1946 British squatters movement,[28] to the mass rent strikes of anti-apartheid resistance in 1980s South Africa.[29] Within contemporary struggles such as the Focus E15 Mothers in Newham, activists are relearning and adapting these tactics, and in doing so often rebuilding lost community.[30]

Towards alternatives

Only a crisis – actual or perceived – produces real change. When that crisis occurs, the actions that are taken depend on the ideas that are lying around. That, I believe, is our basic function: to develop alternatives to existing policies, to keep them alive and available until the politically impossible becomes the politically inevitable.[31]

Milton Friedman

Housing experts and professionals are in agreement: radical change is needed to address the housing crisis. Yet there is no agreed solution.[32] There is an acknowledgement that a sufficient appetite for such change is not going to come anytime soon from the politics of the establishment. Instead, those in power have to be pushed to implement such changes. No foreseeable future government is going to engage in the mass building of social, affordable housing, or regulate the market through the bolstering of tenants' rights or rent controls – not if it negatively affects the profits of landlords or the value of property. It should be no surprise that the wealthy are using the state to further their own material interests. Ultimately, it is going to take mass, sustained and coordinated action to force the government to act against the interests of those currently rich in housing wealth.

We are facing an unprecedented moment in the development of capitalism: nobody really knows where we are heading. Milton Friedman, quoted above, was the most influential free market economist of the twentieth century and a key inspiration for many of those who have intentionally created this situation in housing from the 1970s onwards. He saw opportunity in crisis, opportunity to profit and opportunity to further centralise power in the hands of the wealthy.

What are the alternatives?

In the next sections, we explore alternative models of housing provision, both generally and in specific examples. These ideas are not new and these models will not solve the housing crisis in any immediate sense. But they have the potential to strengthen the wider movement for radical housing reform – and prefigure a better, non-market controlled society.

1. Community Land Trusts

To make housing truly affordable you need to remove it from the market, and you need to remove the ability for people to profit from property. Community Land Trusts are one method for doing this.

Developed in the early 1970s, the modern community land trust movement grew from the American civil rights movement. The aim of the latter was to provide land for landless, often black, southern farmers. Later, this model was also developed and implemented successfully in poor urban areas.[33]

Community Land Trusts are not-for-profit organisations that own land for the primary purpose of providing affordable housing, and for supporting and strengthening a community. The aim is for the land to be owned by the trust forever, so members of the community can affordably lease property on land and avoid the unpredictable fluctuations and disadvantages of the private property market. The trust is democratically controlled by those who live and work in the local area, including tenants of the trust.

One of the first projects in the UK was on Eigg, an island in the Scottish Inner Hebrides. The island was bought by the community in 1997, after problems with absentee landlords, and is now controlled by the community. They have prospered significantly and gone on to create the world's first energy grid that is run solely on renewable energy sources.[34]

2. Co-operative housing

A housing co-operative is a housing provider which is owned and democratically controlled by its tenants, abiding by the co-operative values and principles. Housing co-ops come in many forms, from single households with a handful of tenants, right up to Co-op City in the Bronx, New York, which provides affordable housing to over 55,000 residents, employs over 1000 people and offers a wealth of co-op owned amenities and services.[35]

We have been involved in setting up student housing co-operatives in Edinburgh, Birmingham and Sheffield. Though there are already many housing co-ops across the UK, lack of finance, support and awareness means there has been little growth in the movement. Any movement for co-operative housing for young people is evidently its infancy. Despite this, there are many opportunities for the co-operative model to be applied successfully, as our experiences will show in the following sections.

3. Wider student movement

In 2010, thousands of students from schools, colleges and universities caught the entire British establishment off guard. The National Union of Students, who at the time supported a 'graduate tax', organised a march through Central London against the tripling of tuition fees.

Hundreds of those on the march stormed Millbank Tower, national headquarters of the Conservative Party, to demonstrate their opposition to education cuts, the withdrawal of the Educational Maintenance Allowance, and the tripling of tuition fees to £9000. In losing the immediate fight against the vote in parliament, many were demoralised and demobilised – but were nonetheless politicised. The sense of injustice has left most of us with a distrust of the state, mainstream media, and – in particular – the police. The subsequent movement has formed out of cohorts of students who are battle hardened, stubborn and capable organisers. Participants in this wider student movement are becoming more understanding and critical of the role that wealth plays in their lives.

One offshoot of has been a growing interest in student co-operative ventures: a means of self-help to provide more affordably-run services to one another. Schemes include food co-ops for collectively bulk-buying affordable and healthy food, bike co-ops for cheaply sourcing and repairing bicycles, and swap and re-use hubs for getting cheap, free household goods. Though saving money is a key and much needed attraction, many actively involved students are also driven by the sense of empowerment that co-operatives provide. The spaces which have been formed also function as a location for discussing and mobilising around wider political issues. This has helped to sustain activity through lulls in the student movement.

The largest ventures to date have been student housing co-operatives. Since the end of the nineteenth century there have been many examples of successfully self-managed or partly self-managed student housing. Early experiments include the student-managed University Hall at the University of Edinburgh, founded by polymath Patrick Geddes as part of his attempt to improve Edinburgh's Old Town for its primarily working-class residents.[36] Later projects in the UK and the US were formed to meet the needs of the expanding numbers of women students, such as at the Universities of Wisconsin, Michigan, and Kansas.[37] Many British university student halls were partly self-managed whilst remaining under the authority of the parent institution.

With the Great Depression a number of student housing projects explicitly following co-operative values and principles were established across the US. While affordability was a key motivation, the co-operatives were also organised around issues like peace and anti-racism.

Some early co-ops provided the first racially integrated student housing in the US. Many of the early semi-student-managed halls in Britain had close ties to suffrage campaigners and other political radicals. US-based co-operatives continued to multiply in number, but in Britain, student halls as we know them today became the norm, owned and managed entirely by universities, and more recently by the expanding private halls sector.

4. Edinburgh Student Housing Co-operative

The Edinburgh Student Housing Co-operative has 106 members living in twenty-four flats in two large former university halls, split down the middle by a pub. The co-op is entirely self-managed by the members.

Edinburgh Student Housing Co-operative was established in 2014 following a high-profile on-campus campaign at the University of Edinburgh to oppose high rents and dodgy landlords, and to demonstrate the overwhelming support for affordable student-run alternatives. The campaign built on previous campaigns over the years that had succeeded, for example, the campaign to cap rent increases in the University's student halls. However it was felt that such campaigns could be more easily sustained – and indeed bolstered – by the development of alternative models, which could also be used to inspire and foster wider struggles.

Indeed, it has been much easier to argue for cheaper rent when you can point at the co-operative, charging £305 per month, including all bills – over £100 cheaper than the market rate students would typically pay – making the co-op the city's most affordable student housing provider.

Those of us involved in establishing the co-operative were already actively involved in anti-austerity activism, radical politics, and student unionism. We used these and other networks to mobilise support. The project was helped significantly by the support of a co-operative business consultant, funded by the now decommissioned Co-operative Enterprise Hub, and the elected rector of the university.[38]

Through these networks, support for the idea was secured: within the upper echelons of the University of Edinburgh, who are also one of the city's largest landlords; within Scotmid, the local co-operative retail society and owner of a significant number of properties across our target areas; and at the City of Edinburgh Council. After having offered us a host of brilliant, but unsuitable properties, including derelict factories and a massive brutalist office complex, the Council's Housing Leader recommended us to Castle Rock Edinvar Housing Association (CRE), another of the city's largest landlords, and owner of several suitable properties. In total, it took around eighteen months from developing the initial idea to being handed the hefty boxes of keys.

Initial capital is one of the main barriers to housing co-operatives becoming established. The risks associated with investing or loaning significant amounts in a student housing co-operative – especially when there were no others in the UK – were seen as too high. To avoid the need for up-front capital it was negotiated for the lease to be paid at the end of each quarter, providing time for the co-operative to raise the funds through rent. The lease also allows us to purchase the property once we have secured the finance. Members also paid a £100 membership share, which they received back on leaving the co-operative, raising an initial £10,000.[39] A £15,000 loan and a £2000 grant from Scotmid also helped with cash flow. Set-up costs such as legal fees and building surveyors were charged on sixty day invoices. This set-up led to the bizarre situation whereby on the day we moved in, the co-op had only parted with a total £65 cash!

Co-operatives are not charities, they are about self-help and mutual aid. The co-operative is financially self-sustaining, with the vast bulk of the organisation's income from member rents. The main expenditure is the lease for the property, with other expenditures including electricity, maintenance costs, redevelopment and investment in the property.

As much as possible is managed internally and directly by members. Not only does this save the co-operative significant sums – meaning cheaper rent – but it also helps to strengthen community and empower members. Through working together, members get to know one another, become versed in democratic, participatory and consensus-based organising, and develop a host of new co-op related skills.

The Edinburgh Student Housing Co-operative is part of Students for Cooperation, a network of groups across the UK which attempts to address the desire across the university sector for more democratic student services. Students in Birmingham have also set a housing co-operative with nine bedrooms close to the University, with the financial support of The Phone Co-op, a successful retail co-operative.

Similar plans are afoot in other cities, with Sheffield having almost bought a property under a similar model to that used in Birmingham. Students for Co-operation is working with East of England Co-operative to create a national investment body for student housing co-operatives which will allow us to fund the purchasing of properties so we can establish many more co-operatives across the country.

5. *Role in wider struggles*

For us it is clear that co-operatives are not *the* solution to the housing crisis, but they are one among many. The benefits are not just afford-able housing but providing real examples of democratic self-management. As John Holloway explains: 'The limitations of such co-operatives are clear: in so far as they produce for a market, they are forced to produce under the same conditions as any capitalist enterprise'; in other words, they necessarily reproduce many of the shortcomings of the current system. However if co-operative members work hard to link their resources with other struggles and become part of a wider movement, there is potential to build a movement that moves beyond the current crisis.[40]

To a certain extent these things are already happening. Members of Edinburgh Student Housing Co-operative are involved in the Living Rent Campaign in Scotland; Radical Routes housing co-ops have a long history of supporting social movements. But there is much room for improvement, and much potential. Co-ops are often presented as an economic movement that uses education to further its aims. We'd argue that it should be, first and foremost, an educational movement that uses economics to create spaces of discussion and development. Co-operatives, and other democratic collective solutions to social issues, offer the first sprouts of the new within the old system,[41] a glimpse of what society could be. And co-operatives can also play a role in supporting wider struggles, as they have done at many points throughout history.

Conclusion

Short of revolution, any significant change in the state of housing will require state intervention on a scale not seen since the end of the Second World War: building social housing, heavily regulating the private sector, significantly financing alternative housing models and massively redistributing and socialising housing wealth. But this alone will only mitigate the housing crisis.

There is no isolated solution. The state of housing is fundamentally a symptom of the nature of private property ownership – which goes straight to the foundations of capitalism. This is something that can only be changed through mass collective action across a broad series of fronts. Even trying to extract moderate reform from the state will require mass action – rent strikes, strike action by workers, protests, direct action, and other tactics at our disposal.

We cannot simply hope to slowly collectivise the economy piece by piece – this alone would fail to tackle the underlying systemic issues on which capitalism is built. But we can use such models to strengthen social movements, and to prepare people to truly take direct collective, democratic control over the economy, society, and ultimately, our lives.

If you want to be happy
In the name of God,
Hang your landlord!
—Le Père Duchesne

Sean Farmelo is a Network Co-ordinator for Students For Co-operation. As a student in Birmingham he helped to found the Green Bike Project and the Birmingham Student Housing Co-operative. Sean is an editor of Slaney Street – a co-operative newspaper, and a member of Plan C. He campaigns on social issues and is a bicycle instructor.

Mike Shaw is a Network Co-ordinator for Students for Co-operation, and a co-founder of Edinburgh Student Housing Co-operative. He has been an active organiser for Edinburgh University Anti-Cuts Coalition, Edinburgh University Students' Association, Edinburgh University Socialist Society and the National Campaign Against Fees and Cuts.

Notes

1. 'Food Costs: "£50 Chickens" If Food Tracked House Prices'. *BBC News*, 7 February 2013. http://www.bbc.co.uk/news/business-21365920.
2. Bethan Thomas, and Danny Dorling, *Know Your Place – Housing Wealth*

and Inequality in Great Britain 1980-2003 and beyond, London, 2004. http://www.sasi.group.shef.ac.uk/publications/reports/Knowyourplace.pdf.

3. Kate Allen, 'Home Buyers Left behind in Britain's Two-Speed Housing Market', *Financial Times*, 17 January 2014. http://www.ft.com/cms/s/0/ea516116-7f92-11e3-94d2-00144feabdc0.html#axzz3Llcv3vIQ.

4. Christopher Hope, 'Villagers "under siege" from aggressive developers after planning reforms, say MPs', *The Telegraph*, 16 December 2014. http://www.telegraph.co.uk/news/earth/greenpolitics/planning/11295380/Villagers-under-siege-from-aggressive-developers-after-planning-reforms-say-MPs.html.

5. Claire Crawford, and Wenchao Ji, *Payback Time?: Student Debt and Loan Repayments: What Will the 2012 Reforms Mean for Graduates?* The Sutton Trust, 10 April 2014. http://www.suttontrust.com/researcharchive/payback-time/.

6. OECD, 'A Family Affair', in *Economic Policy Reforms*, pp. 181–98, Organisation for Economic Co-operation and Development, 2010. http://www.oecd-ilibrary.org/content/chapter/growth-2010-38-en.

7. Patrick Collinson, 'House Prices: Guide to Property Hotspots', *The Guardian*, 30 March 2012, sec. Money. http://www.theguardian.com/money/2012/mar/30/house-prices-guide-proerty-hotspots.

8. Wendy Wilson, *Housing Supply and Demand*, Briefing paper, London: House of Commons, 2010. http://www.parliament.uk/business/publications/research/key-issues-for-the-new-parliament/social-reform/housing-supply-and-demand/.

9. Steve Wilcox, John Perry, and Peter Williams, *UK Housing Review 2014 Briefing Paper*, The Chartered Institute of Housing, 25 June 2014. http://www.cih.org/resources/PDF/Policy%20free%20download%20pdfs/UKHR%20Briefing%202014%20bookmarked.pdf.

10. Hugh Bochel, and Guy Daly, ed, *Social Policy*, London, 2014, p. 385.

11. David Kingman, *Why BTL Equals 'Big Tax Let-Off': How the UK Tax System Hands Buy-to-Let Landlords an Unfair Advantage*, Intergenerational Foundation, 25 November 2013. http://www.if.org.uk/archives/4668/tax-payers-fund-5-billion-annual-buy-to-let-tax-write-offs.

12. Steve Wilco, *A Financial Evaluation of the Right to Buy*, The Welsh Assembly, September 2006. http://www.assembly.wales/NAfW%20Documents/ah9_-_professor_steve_wilcox.pdf%20-%2005022008/ah9_-_professor_steve_wilcox-English.pdf.

13. Pete Apps, 'Report Finds 52,000 Right to Buy Homes in London Now Rented Privately', *Inside Housing*, 13 January 2014. http://www.insidehousing.co.uk/report-finds-52000-right-to-buy-homes-in-london-now-rented-privately/7001600.article.

14. 'Landlords Bible: Grounds for Possession by a Landlord of Their Rental Property', *PropertyHawk*. Accessed 6 March 2015. http://www.property-hawk.co.uk/?grounds-for-possession.

15. Kevin Gulliver, 'Thatcher's Legacy: Her Role in Today's Housing Crisis',

The Guardian, 17 April 2013. http://www.theguardian.com/housing-network/2013/apr/17/margaret-thatcher-legacy-housing-crisis.

16. John Bibby, '2013/14: The Worst Year for Social Rented House Building since WW2', *Shelter Policy Blog*, 23 October 2014. http://blog.shelter.org.uk/2014/10/201314-the-worst-year-for-social-rented-house-building-since-ww2/.

17. John Bibby, 'In 60 per cent of the Country, Social House Building Has Effectively Stopped', *Shelter Policy Blog*, 13 November 2014. http://blog.shelter.org.uk/2014/11/in-60-of-the-country-social-house-building-has-effectively-stopped/.

18. Andrew Fisher, 'London's Housing Crisis Hotspots', *The Guardian*, 22 August 2012. http://www.theguardian.com/news/datablog/2012/aug/22/housingmarket-london-data.

19. John Perry, 'Who Really Gets Government Subsidised Housing?'. *The Guardian*, 27 January 2012, sec. Housing Network. http://www.theguardian.com/housing-network/2012/jan/27/government-subsidised-social-housing-rent.

20. Suzanne Fitzpatrick, Hal Pawson, Glen Bramley, Steve Wilcox, and Beth Watts, *The Homelessness Monitor: England 2013*. Institute for Housing, Urban and Real Estate Research, Heriot-Watt University; Centre for Housing Policy, University of York; City Futures Research Centre, University of New South Wales, December 2013. http://www.crisis.org.uk/data/files/publications/HomelessnessMonitorEngland2013.pdf.

21. 'Mark Fortune Update: Edinburgh's Worst Landlord Still In Business After Council Ban', *Edinburgh Private Tenants Action Group*, 6 December 2013.http://eptag.org.uk/2013/12/mark-fortune-update-edinburghs-worst-landlord-still-in-business-after-council-ban/.

22. Michael Byers, 'Red Clydeside: A History of the Labour Movement in Glasgow 1910-1932'. *Glasgow Digital Library*. Accessed 6 March 2015. http://gdl.cdlr.strath.ac.uk/redclyde/.

23. Michael Byers, 'The Singer Strike 1911'. *Red Clydeside: A History of the Labour Movement in Glasgow 1910-1932*. http://sites.scran.ac.uk/redclyde/redclyde/docs/rcpeomarybarbour.htm.

24. Michael Byers, 'Mary Barbour (1875-1958)'. *Red Clydeside: A History of the Labour Movement in Glasgow 1910-1932*, n.d. http://sites.scran.ac.uk/redclyde/redclyde/rceve1.htm.

25. Narrow lanes between houses.

26. John Couzin, *Radical Glasgow: A Skeletal Sketch of Glasgow's Radical Tradition*. Glasgow: Voline Press, 2006. http://www2.gcu.ac.uk/radicalglasgow/chapters/rent_strikes.html.

27. Wendy Wilson, *The Historical Context of Rent Control in the Private Rented Sector*. Briefing paper. London: House of Commons, 5 March 2014. http://www.parliament.uk/business/publications/research/briefing-papers/SN06747/the-historical-context-of-rent-control-in-the-private-rented-sector.

28. Colin Ward, *The Hidden History of Housing*. Policy paper. History & Policy, 1 September 2004. http://www.historyandpolicy.org/index.php/ policy-papers/papers/the-hidden-history-of-housing.

29. 'The People Armed, 1984-1990'. *South African History Online*. Accessed 6 March 2015. http://www.sahistory.org.za/liberation-struggle-south-africa/people-armed-1984-1990.

30. Aditya Chakrabortty. 'For Real Politics, Don't Look to Parliament but to an Empty London Housing Estate', *The Guardian*, 23 September 2014. http://www.theguardian.com/commentisfree/2014/sep/23/ real-politics-empty-london-housing-estate.

31. Milton Friedman, *Capitalism and Freedom*, Chicago, 1982, p. 7.

32. Tom de Castella, 'Eight Radical Solutions to the Housing Crisis', *BBC News*, 25 October 2011. http://www.bbc.co.uk/news/magazine-15400477.

33. John Emmeus Davis, 'Origins and Evolution of the Community Land Trust in the United States (2010)', in *The Community Land Trust Reader*, pp. 3-47. Cambridge: Lincoln Institute of Land Policy, 2010.

34. Alistair Munro, 'Eigg Islanders Observe 16 Years of Community Buyout', *The Scotsman*, 12 June 2013. http://www.scotsman.com/news/scotland/top-stories/eigg-islanders-observe-16-years-of-community-buyout-1-2963314.

35. Elsa Brenner, 'Everything You Need, in One Giant Package', *The New York Times*, 6 April 2008, sec. Real Estate. http://www.nytimes. com/2008/04/06/realestate/06live.html.

36. 'Patrick Geddes (1854-1932)', *National Library of Scotland*, n.d. http:// www.nls.uk/learning-zone/politics-and-society/patrick-geddes.

37. Deborah Altus, 'A Look at Student Housing Cooperatives', *Fellowship for Intentional Community*. Accessed 6 March 2015. http://www.ic.org/wiki/ look-student-housing-cooperatives/.

38. The Rector is a role unique to Scotland's 'Ancient' universities. The Rector is elected by students and staff to chair the university's governing body and represent their interests to university management.

39. Unlike a deposit, which legally must be kept in a third party deposit holding scheme, the co-operative has no right to deduct costs for damages from the share.

40. John Holloway, *Change the World without Taking Power*, London, 2005, p. 240.

41. Karl Marx, 'Chapter 27. The Role of Credit in Capitalist Production', in *Capital Volume III Part V Division of Profit into Interest and Profit of Enterprise. Interest-Bearing Capital*. USSR: Institute of Marxism-Leninism, 1894. https://www.marxists.org/archive/marx/works/1894-c3/ch27.htm.

Focus E15 and Aylesbury: squatting against London's housing crisis

Izzy Köksal

Within the last year, housing struggles in London have grown in number and visibility. Even the mainstream media is taking an interest, with coverage ranging from 'Protesters disrupt London property fair', in *The Guardian*, to 'SQUAT A CHEEK' in *The Sun*.

Direct action tactics are key to the vibrancy and effectiveness of these new housing campaigns. Already the first two months of 2015 have seen a 2000 strong 'March for Homes' to City Hall, led by Focus E15 mums. Despite relentless cold and rain, the march was joined by a large number of local community groups and individuals. About 100 people pelted bailiffs with paint-bombs, as they made their way to an awards ceremony, having to navigate the 'mock eviction' site the protesters had constructed at the entrance. There have also been two protest occupations in south London, including, as explored later in this chapter, on the Aylesbury housing estate in Elephant and Castle.

These increasingly co-ordinated actions are a push back against the housing crisis that is currently affecting London and the rest of the UK. Housing groups and campaigns are proliferating, linked together through the Radical Housing Network and London Coalition Against Poverty. Soaring private rents, cuts to housing benefits and welfare more generally, and the demolition of council estates as part of 'regeneration' schemes, are just some of the ways that the government and their developer friends are causing homelessness, displacement and the deepening impoverishment of working class communities. High rents mean that poor people have found themselves forced further and further out of London. The Localism Act 2012 took this a step further, giving local councils the powers to forcibly send homeless residents out of London, in what might be termed state-led social cleansing.

Focus E15 mums, New Era, and Our West Hendon are three women-led housing campaigns that have used direct action to gain actual successes, wide support and mainstream media attention in the last year. The London Coalition Against Poverty, running since 2007, is also predominantly organised by women, mostly women of colour, who provide mutual support and take collective action on housing and benefit issues.

In September 2012, perhaps in anticipation of rising homelessness as a result of welfare and housing cuts, the government made squatting in a residential property a criminal offence under section 144 of the Legal Aid, Sentencing and Punishment of Offenders Act. The wording of the new law makes it a criminal offence if 'the person is living in the [residential] building or intends to live there for any period'. Squatters and housing campaigners are challenging this new law – and the actions of councils, housing associations and owners – by organising protest occupations, with rotas to prove that no-one is living or intending to live in the building. Housing Action Southwark and Lambeth organised the first protest occupation in a residential building in October 2013. They occupied 'Britain's most expensive council house',[1] worth £2.96 million, in protest at its sell-off and the wider sell-off of council housing.

Focus E15 Mums

In early 2014, a group of under twenty-five year-old single mothers were served eviction notices from the Focus E15 hostel in which they were living. Newham council told them it would rehouse them in private accommodation in Manchester, Hastings and Birmingham. This would have forced the young mothers to leave their communities and support networks. The group, who became known as Focus E15 mums, refused to accept this and kicked off their resistance campaign by organising occupations of the Focus E15 offices and the council offices.

By September 2014, they had occupied four empty flats on the Carpenter Estate in Stratford, campaigning under the slogan 'social housing not social cleansing'. Their protests saw Newham council back down and offer them private accommodation in the borough. They are continuing their campaign for local, social housing for everyone who needs it, and regularly support others with housing problems, organising eviction resistances and mass visits to the housing office.

The Carpenters estate is in the process of being 'decanted' by the council, who were hoping to capitalise on the Olympics by selling off the land to private developers. Many of the houses on the estate have been left empty for years. The Focus E15 mums had been told there was no social housing for them in Newham. But on the estate they found hundreds of decent, council homes that the council were leaving to rot. Their occupation of the abandoned flats, supported by squatters, highlighted Newham council's role in the housing crisis. It's not that there is a shortage of homes, but that councils and the government aren't interested in providing homes for poor people. They would prefer to leave the homes empty and send homeless people to other cities. The banners across the occupied houses conveyed Focus E15's simple message: 'These people need homes, these homes need people'.

The four squatted houses were opened as a social centre for locals on the Carpenters estate and for supporters from across London. A programme of activities included film screenings, meetings, workshops, and open mic nights. Children played games outside in the yard. The children-oriented nature of the protest was a welcome change from most protests. The protest occupation threw national media attention onto the campaign, and importantly, onto the housing polices of Newham council. Momentum built around the occupation. Despite Newham council attempting to turn the water off (but actually just 'mashing up the pipes'),[2] employing security guards to patrol the estate to intimate the protesters, and lying to the media about the campaign,[3] Newham council were forced to concede to the Focus E15 mums.[4] In court, the council, who had been trying to get an Interim Possession Order (IPO) for the flats, agreed that the women could leave on an agreed date. It also announced that it would be making forty of the flats available as temporary accommodation to homeless people – although the Focus E15 campaign is demanding the repopulation of the estate with secure council tenancies.

The Focus E15 squatted occupation created an accessible protest space for people of a wide range of ages. It helped to make links with residents on the estate, especially those who are also facing displacement. It attracted significant media attention, with the dubious honour of being covered by Russell Brand on 'The Trews'. Most of all, it was a key example of how the law to criminalise squatting in residential buildings can be challenged. The occupation even managed to win the civil proceedings in court when the council decided against the use of an IPO.

The Aylesbury occupation

Located in Elephant and Castle, south London, the Aylesbury estate is in the process of being 'decanted': like the Carpenters and like the Heygate estate before it. It is part of a scheme that will see a loss of council homes and an increase in private, unaffordable flats. Residents on the Aylesbury voted in a ballot in 2001 against being transferred from council ownership to ownership by a housing association, but this ballot is not being honoured.[5] As resident Rob Mitchell put it: 'They're all fucking liars and I'm not voting for anyone until they fix the lifts'. This quote is now a banner hanging from the occupation.

Squatters occupied a block on the Aylesbury estate after the March for Homes on 31 January 2015. The protest occupation is in solidarity with residents on the Aylesbury, against the social cleansing and gentrification that the 'regeneration' of the estate will facilitate. As a squatting action, it challenges the criminalisation of squatting. In a statement, the occupiers – perhaps incriminatingly – state:

> Squatting was criminalised at the same time as estates were being destroyed all over London. At Aylesbury we find a struggle like our own: a fight against eviction and for space in which we can not only survive but really live. Squatters and tenants unite![6]

The Aylesbury protest occupation has run daily, well-attended meetings for occupiers, tenants and supporters and has attempted to open up the space for people to use. Unlike the flats on the Carpenters estate where there was running hot water and electricity, Southwark council had spent money destroying the bathrooms, to prevent occupation and use of the flats. The squatters put in a great deal of time and energy making the flats barely habitable. Police patrolling and harassment also meant that it was not always possible to make the occupation easily accessible. Despite these obstacles, the occupation still managed to organise a number of events, including a football tournament, a fun day, and a protest where they returned parts of the smashed up Aylesbury to Southwark council's town hall. Local tenants' groups and housing groups have signed a statement in support of the squatters, and a number of Aylesbury residents have brought the squatters donations, including pots of hot soup.

'*The Guardian* don't like us because we're not single mums', one occupier commented as they reflected on the lack of media interest for this occupation – not that *The Guardian* are necessarily good friends to single mums either. But it is only the mainstream media making dividing lines between the two occupations and their occupiers. Like the Focus E15 mums, the people involved in the Aylesbury are mostly young people who struggle with, and against, precarious living conditions. They write: 'We are the generation who has nothing to defend: no council housing and no homes we own, no sense of belonging to any place, just endless badly paid, insecure, dead-end work'.[7] With David Cameron's pre-election announcement of further cuts to housing benefit for young people, and promises of more workfare, the future could be even bleaker.

Southwark council and the police responded to the occupation with harassment, perhaps feeling they could get away with intimidating squatters. Shortly into the occupation, another block was occupied but illegally evicted by Southwark council officials and the police.[8] The council hired private security to wait at the entrance of a new occupation, and currently three 'dog unit' vans are parked up outside.[9] The council have also begun to erect half-complete metal fences around the Aylesbury estate where the occupation and residents are still living. In effect, the squatters have spent weeks under siege.

The council took the squatters to court on 17 February 2015 and won an IPO. This was something of a victory, as the residential squatting law was not used and the council had to take action through the civil courts. But a violent eviction followed later that evening, with 100 riot cops invading the part of the estate where the occupation was held, violently arresting supporters and one resident. The Focus E15 mums campaign were there that night, showing support. While the eviction was occurring, another block was occupied by the squatters. It was only because of the brutality of the eviction that the mainstream media paid any attention to the protest occupation.

The squatters have made it clear that they will stay for as long as they can, doing their best under the circumstances to engage with residents and locals, to show resistance to Southwark council's disastrous housing policies and to squat as a way – they say – 'to take control over our lives'.[10]

Direct action

Arising out of women's immediate housing needs, these and similar campaigns have subsequently widened their scope, demanding quality, secure social housing for everyone. Our West Hendon explain the importance of direct action:

> Every temporary tenant granted a secure or even a flexible tenancy in the local community is a great victory for Our West Hendon. Sadly today we saw a lady who has not been involved in our campaigns. She was being moved from her temporary tenancy to yet another temporary tenancy on Graham Park, with her kids. Forced to travel four miles to school every day. We believe direct action works but you got to be part of it to benefit from it! Barnet Homes say they aren't moving temporary tenants to further temporary tenancies, we know this is a lie and today we caught the truth on camera ... [11]

In this way, working-class women, who are directly affected by homelessness and bad, precarious housing, are at the forefront of fighting back. They are under no illusion that the government or local council are interested in their lives. Stopping an eviction or preventing someone from being forced out of London by the local council requires immediate action. These occupations allowed for cross-tenure organising, solidarity, skill sharing, and important open meeting spaces.

The Carpenter's and Aylesbury estate protest occupations got to the core of the 'housing crisis' by taking back exactly what is needed. They showed that the criminalisation of squatting in empty residential buildings can be successfully challenged. They made the problem visible. By opening up spaces, they allowed people to meet, plan and even live for some time. The occupations forced the local councils to address the issues raised, albeit with lies and misinformation.

The occupations are part of a wave of organising around housing happening now across London and the UK. The growing co-ordination between groups, the familiarity and friendships, infrastructure building, knowledge and tactic sharing, the increased number of militant actions, and the amount of people attending them point to the beginnings of a housing movement in London. As the Focus E15 mums said: 'This is the beginning of the end of the housing crisis'.

Izzy Köksal organises on housing and welfare with Housing Action Southwark and Lambeth, Boycott Workfare, and the London Coalition Against Poverty.

Notes

1. Adam Withnall, 'Squatters occupy Britain's most expensive council on day it sells for £2.96m', *The Independent*, 29 October 2013. http://www.independent.co.uk/news/uk/home-news/squatters-occupy-britains-most-expensive-council-house-on-day-it-sells-for-296m-8911319.html

2. Zoe Williams, 'Housing: how many have to be unable to afford it before it becomes a political problem?', *The Guardian*, 26 September 2014. http://www.theguardian.com/society/2014/sep/26/housing-east-london-estate-viability-affordability

3. Councillor Andrew Baikie described the women as 'agitators and hangers-on', stated that the women had been helped to find accommodation in Newham or wider London (this was only after their protests), and claimed that 'the needs of the wider people of Newham are being ignored for the sake of petty, expensive stunts'. http://www.newham.gov.uk/Pages/News/Response-to-recent-news-coverage-about-the-Carpenters-Estate.aspx

4. Esther Addley, 'Newham council drops plans to evict housing campaigners in twenty-four hours', *The Guardian*, 2 October 2014. http://www.theguardian.com/uk-news/2014/oct/02/newham-council-drops-plans-evict-focus-e15-housing-campaigners-east-london

5. 'Southwark housing campaigns and activists support the occupation on the Aylesbury Estate', Southwark Notes – whose regeneration? 6 Feburary 2015.https://southwarknotes.wordpress.com/2015/02/06/southwark-housing-campaigns-and-activists-support-the-occupation-on-the-aylesbury-estate/

6. 'Statement from the Aylesbury Estate occupation', Fight for the Aylesbury, 1 February 2015. https://fightfortheaylesbury.wordpress.com/2015/02/01/statement-from-the-*aylesbury*-estate-occupation/

7. 'Squat the lot', Fight for the Aylesbury, 20 Feburary 2015. https://fightfortheaylesbury.wordpress.com/2015/02/20/squat-the-lot/

8. 'Southwark council and police smash up eight empty homes trying to stop occupation spreading', Fight for the Aylesbury, 5 February 2015. https://fightfortheaylesbury.wordpress.com/2015/02/05/southwark-council-and-police-smash-up-8-empty-homes-trying-to-stop-occupation-spreading/

9. 'Security pests start lurking in the Aylesbury Bushes', Fight for the Aylesbury, 20 February 2015. https://fightfortheaylesbury.wordpress.com/2015/02/20/security-pests-start-lurking-in-the-ayeslbury-bushes/

10. 'Squat the lot', Fight for the Aylesbury, 20 Feburary 2015. https://fightfortheaylesbury.wordpress.com/2015/02/20/squat-the-lot/

11. Our West Hendon Facebook page, dated 11 December 2014.

Scotland's referendum and the politics of the future

Niki Seth-Smith

What I'm about to argue shouldn't be controversial. Namely, that the 2014 Scottish independence referendum was the most important political event yet for my generation of young people in Britain. Not only that: it was a harbinger of the kind of politics we can expect for the future, not only in the UK but also Europe-wide. The independence campaign was movement-based, created alliances across political tribes and the vote was direct democracy in action, if not of the radical kind. In a country whose political system has been dying of slow suffocation – with the average voting age rising and increasing numbers turning their backs on the ballot box – it re-engaged the 'missing million', including 80 per cent of under thirty-fives. The majority of these young people voted for independence. In fact, without the country's pensioners, who voted against by 77 per cent, Scotland would now be an independent country. The 'impossible', the end of Britain as we know it, very nearly happened, falling short by a 10 per cent gap.

A movement for democracy

I was lucky enough to be staying in East Lothian, near Edinburgh, in the three months leading up to Scotland's referendum on 18 September 2014. Nothing prepared me for walking the streets of Edinburgh and Glasgow during that time. This was not a campaign controlled by Alex Salmond, the First Minister of Scotland and leader of the ruling Scottish National Party (SNP), as much of the coverage coming out of the London-based media would have had us believe. The independence movement was a broad alliance, overlapping but not dominated by the 'official' Yes campaign (itself a cross-party body but, as you might expect, heavily steered by the Scottish government). When asked about the party 'breakdown' of the movement, it would be fair to say it was mainly SNP, Green, Scottish Socialist Party and some Labour supporters, but this would be missing the point. A staggering number of people in Scotland took some part in the referendum campaigns, from either side, although the Yes campaign's activist base was far larger. Reflective of the general population, the majority of these 'activists' were not party members and did not self-define along party lines.

I am not going to deal here with the many and complex reasons why, as a young English woman, I voted 'Yes' to Scotland breaking away from the British state. You do not have to agree with my position to recognise that the kind of politics the referendum generated can be placed in a continuum with other movements for democracy and political rejuvenation over the last half decade, movements that have been clearly framed as 'youth politics'. Why not the Scottish referendum? The fact that it carried the spirit of the 2011-2012 wave of social movements, including Occupy, the Indignados and what was then called the Arab Spring, should have been clear from the start, and not simply because a significant number of young people voting 'Yes' in Scotland described their political journey explicitly in those terms.

Crucially, the referendum gave young people the chance to challenge the nature of the democratic system, not just to place an X in a box. Again, we won't dig into the arguments around how deliverable this promise was. Suffice to say that those voting 'Yes' were backing more and deeper democracy. This was most obvious at the national level; they sought to bring power closer to the 5 million people living in Scotland and to boot out the Tories that Scotland never voted in. But the independence movement outside of the SNP also emphasised the opportunities for delivering more radical proposals for local, decentralised decision-making. An important example is Common Weal's 'people's manifesto', a key document for the wider movement, which advocates for policy to be driven by mini-publics, through mechanisms such as citizen assemblies and deliberative polls. If the referendum had been about a narrow nationalistic 'right' to home rule, a silence would now reign over Scotland. Instead, in the fortnight after the 'No' vote, both the Greens and SNP's membership tripled, while Common Weal and the Radical Independence Campaign are realigning their strategies for the May 2015 General Elections.

Building a genuinely politically engaged citizenry required only one action: asking a question with genuine consequences for people's lives. It was something that my generation of young people in Britain had never experienced.

When it was announced that sixteen and seventeen year-olds would be given the vote, the first polls confirmed the idea that Scottish teenagers would vote to stay in Britain. Alex Salmond had made a big mistake, the commentators said: of course, young people were against 'nationalism', 'separatism' and the nostalgic, romantic idea of 'freedom from the London yoke'. Even Ian Bell, columnist for the Scottish Herald, the only newspaper in the UK to support independence, published an apologetic letter to 'Young Scotland' after the vote. 'I had assumed that you don't fight a referendum with kids', he admitted, 'But they were, always, the best of us'. Commentators across the board profoundly misunderstood the independence movement, which won over these teenagers, ending with over 90 per cent registering to vote, and 71 per cent voting 'Yes'. I don't believe they would have been brought over if my generation, Generation Y, had not led from the front, using social media and 'boots on the ground', events and direct action, to engage this younger demographic. Back in late 2013, Ipsos Mori brought out a report on what they called the 'Independence Generation'. They found that Generation Y, those born in the 1980s and 1990s, were far more likely to vote for an independent Scotland. By referendum day, nearly a year later, this generation had been joined by the sixteen and seventeen year-olds, newly given the vote, along with those aged between thirty-five and sixty-five. Pensioners, consuming anti-independence newspapers and TV and largely absent from social media, were just too difficult for the independence movement to reach.

Why did this generational dynamic come as a surprise? My theory is that, on a fundamental level, young people like myself are presumed to be 'global' in our outlook and thus uninterested in the 'national'. Anyone under thirty-five has grown up during an era of slow and apparently inevitable dissolution, with the 'nation' weakening along with national democracy. Why would we care about either? During our lives, trans-nationals, NGOs and international governing bodies have expanded their powers, as has the European Union, without strengthening its own forms of democracy. The system of representational democracy has become increasingly unstable and compromised, but nothing has been seriously proposed to replace it. Yet, as we saw with the 2011-2012 social movements, despair at the democratic system can lead to engagement with changing this system. Is it so inconceivable that the same trend might apply to national politics? Yet we find it hard to accept that young people might be interested in redefining and redrawing their national political communities. Rather than seeing this as the next step of endeavouring to claim agency over our national democracies, we at once cry 'nationalism', presuming to find patriotic sentiments of racial and cultural supremacy underlying such a politics.

Young people and the 'death of the nation'

It is clear that Scotland's young people are not, all of a sudden, majority 'nationalists' in the sense described above. In fact, polling in the week before the vote found that those voting 'No' cited 'national identity' as one of their three main reasons for doing so, while identity did not appear in the polling of those intending to vote 'Yes'. This indicates that a weakening of 'British' identity could have been more of a factor for those supporting Scottish independence than a strengthening of 'Scottish' identity. In turn, this reflects a broader UK-wide trend that has seen younger demographics identifying less strongly with 'Britishness' over the years. Leaving aside Northern Ireland with its sectarian divisions along Republican and Loyalist lines, young people in Scotland and Wales are more likely to identify as only Scottish or Welsh, not British. Perhaps more surprisingly, under thirty-fives in England are more likely to want more powers for England.

Through this framework, the picture of young people's relationship to the nation within the British Isles takes on a new shape. Much has been made of a recent Ipsos Mori report that appeared to find that Generation Y was less supportive of the welfare state than older generations. But the report explicitly warns against such a conclusion, pointing out that there has been a cross-generational fall in support for spending on welfare, while the most marked generational difference is over the statement: 'the creation of the welfare state is one of Britain's proudest achievements'. Eighteen to twenty-five year olds were the least likely to agree with this, while very high levels answered 'don't know'.

This could be read as lack of support for the welfare state, or ambivalence towards the ideas of 'Britishness' and of 'British pride'. Last year, research by the Economist Intelligence Unit into the democratic health of countries across the globe concluded that Britain is 'beset by a deep institutional crisis' with 'trust in government, parliament and politicians at an all-time low'. As the same Ipsos Mori report found, this is particularly true of younger generations, who 'tend to value personal choice more, and traditional institutions less'. To say that this marks Generation Y as a 'selfish' or 'individualistic' generation is to confuse the traditional institutions of the British state with effective, benevolent bodies that accommodate the desires and needs of all British citizens, or indeed that treat the citizens of all nations in any way equally.

To put it bluntly, us 'Millenials', 'Thatcher's children', 'Generation Net', have little concrete experience of Britain as a functioning national community of politics and solidarity. Falling party and trade union memberships have marked our political lifetimes: institutions that once linked politics across borders. We have grown up under a devolution settlement, watching the post-war consensus of the welfare state and public services being dismantled, shrunk, asset stripped or sold off to the private sector. Many young people in Scotland and Wales observe what is taking place in England with horror, and see their national politicians struggling to use their devolved powers to soften the sharper edges of austerity. While Thatcher never dared to touch the health service, the NHS of England and Wales is now divided between state and private service providers, making creeping privatisation one of the key fears pushing people in Scotland to vote in favour of breaking away from Westminster. The drift between the nations of Britain is set to continue, regardless of the 'No' vote in the Scottish referendum.

Over the next decade, it will become increasingly important not to get trapped in a London mentality, which sees movements for self-determination in Britain's regions and nations as 'nationalistic' (meaning patriotic and supremacist) or 'parochial'. British identity is far stronger in London: the capital and Birmingham are the only regions in the UK where over 30 per cent of people identify as only British. A strong feeling of 'Britishness' is now the exception, not the rule, particularly for young people. This does not only concern Scotland, Wales and Northern Ireland, but England too. The think tank IPPR has done a lot of work on the emergence of a politics of Englishness over the last two years and the way in which the Scottish independence referendum has reinforced this trend. The majority of people living in England now want more powers over their country, with polls suggesting younger generations feel slightly more strongly about the need for English democracy. In *The Politics of English Nationhood*, Michael Kenny explains the rising support for reforming English democracy as linked to 'a return across Europe to forms of belonging associated with historic forms of national and regional identity'. But are young people articulating a stronger sense of identity and 'belonging' than older generations? The general trends common to Generation X and Y might suggest that this is more to do with power and voice: in other words a democratic demand.

It is understandably worrying to the political establishments of our countries that young people's politics may not be as 'global' in outlook as it first may seem. Occupy, certainly in its British manifestation, fitted a particular narrative that can be seen as running parallel to that of neoliberal individualism: that of individuals empowered by technological innovation, in global leaderless networks (just like markets), fostering a kind of borderless form of political identity that left no institutional legacy that could have allowed it to build beyond this. I felt myself to be part of, and am supportive of Occupy, and of course it was (and is) something more than this. The 99 per cent slogan is one of trans-national solidarity, recognising that economic inequality and exploitation, exacerbated and brought into sharp relief by the financial crash, is a global problem requiring a global solution. This is not only a correct analysis, but the only possible moral response to the state of the world today. This does not mean that the 'Umbrella Revolution' in Hong Kong, drawing heavily on student politics and initiated by a group called Occupy Central, cannot advocate global solidarity while focusing its agency on the Chinese and Hong Kong political systems. Would this be any less a movement with a global consciousness and outlook, if it were to advocate the separation of Hong Kong from China as the only way to ensure free and fair elections of nominated and directly elected candidates without interference from the Communist Party of China?

A politics for the future

To take a step back, the politics that emerged around Scottish independence should be seen alongside so-called 'networked' and 'globally-minded' social movements like Occupy in its many manifestations. There is less contradiction here than there might at first appear. The independence movement put great emphasis on a 'Yes' vote as the internationalist choice. The removal of Trident was a reason in itself to many voters, but a 'Yes' vote was also positioned as heralding a move away from foreign aggression and militarism. In the longer-term, breaking away from Britain would guarantee that Scotland would remain in the European Union. The internationalist vision of the 'Yes' movement was a powerful rallying call for Generation Y, many of whom were politicised by the 2 million anti-Iraq march in 2003 and its dismissal by the Blair government. Across Britain, Generations X and Y are more pro-European than older demographics, and have arguably more to lose with the prospect of an end to free movement across European borders and the ability to work, live and study on the continent with comparative ease.

In a recent article, the journalist and author Paul Mason calls Scotland and Catalonia 'straws in the wind for the whole of Europe'. He points to recent OECD predictions for the next fifty years, which see the economies of European countries slowing and stagnating unless two main changes occur: mass inward migration to balance ageing populations; and state-directed innovation that 'ideally solves the energy problem'. He argues that big states will find this difficult to do, hence the rationale for small-state separation. 'It is not just that big states are unwieldy', he says. 'Old developed countries such as Britain and Spain have political elites aligned with economic interests that do not favour state-funded innovation, high immigration or sustainable energy'. The SNP's White Paper, their 'blueprint for independence', placed a great deal of emphasis on encouraging skilled migrants to settle, while their economic programme promised state investment and the development of a 'new green economy'. Much of the wider independence movement went further in proposals for more radical environmental policy and the further opening of Scottish borders. Whether you agree with the 'Yes' campaign or not, that it presented a long-term vision for the future cannot be denied. It is not surprising that young people should vote for the promise of a politics that is vocal about combatting long-term problems and preventing future crises, which they may see in their lifetimes.

Much fun has been poked at supporters of Scottish independence through comparisons between Alex Salmond and Nigel Farage (both are strong, charismatic figures, both want state autonomy and the repatriation of powers). However, many 'Yes' voters saw independence as a way to break free from a country defined by UKIP's vision of the future.

UKIP, an anti-immigration party, reliant on a battalion of grey votes, with its pathological hatred of wind farms and all things 'green', is short-term politics at its most dangerous. The Westminster political class are at once fascinated by UKIP and over-willing to bend over backwards to bring back their older voters, exacerbating a vicious cycle of youth disengagement. The fact that young people are in general repelled by UKIP's politics of ethnic nationalism – reliant on nostalgia, intolerance and the desire for ethnic and cultural purity – is a reason to be hopeful for Britain's future.

A major factor is that Generations X and Y reflect the general trend of a decrease in deference to authority, tradition and hierarchy. We are not searching for a 'lost Britain' that we have never known. It is also a positive rejection, in which the Scottish referendum played a part, of a politics of hatred and fear, one that inevitably arises in times of financial hardship and unease. We can't rely on this forever. The majority of young people in Britain believe they will be 'worse off than their parents'. Under thirty-fives, disproportionately under- and un-employed, with squeezed wages, in rented accommodation and leading precarious lives, could yet prove good hunting ground for Nigel Farage. Surely, this group also needs a scapegoat to explain the sudden change in their fortunes, caused by economic and socio-political global factors that are overwhelming in their complexity? In Matthew Goodwin's book *Revolt on the Right* he identifies UKIP's voter base as built on the 'left-behind' social groups. These are mainly old, white, working-class and lower middle-class males. Only 15 per cent of UKIP members are under forty. Yet young people in Britain today also face uncertainties as to their identity and role in society.

This brings us to the overall vision of an independent Scotland as presented by the movement: that of a 'fairer' and 'more equal' society. Again, we won't deal here with how deliverable this vision was, but only with the kind of political alliance it inspired, between voters from lower income groups, and voters from lower age groups. Under thirty-fives have suffered disproportionately at the hands of the austerity program implemented following the 2008 financial crash, so younger demographics would inevitably be more willing to take risks with the economy in order to combat growing inequality and desperation, a perspective that would be shared with the most vulnerable members of all age groups. Immigrant communities were also more likely to vote Yes. This aligns loosely with the composition of the 'precariat' as set out in Guy Standing's book, *The Precariat: The New Dangerous Class*. Standing envisions an emerging group with shared interests, spanning the unemployed and under-employed young, the 'graduate without a future', the migrant population and communities formerly belonging to the traditional working class. Standing references Occupy within his analysis of an emerging politics of the precariat, but much of this discourse could equally be applied to the movement for Scottish independence. 'Youth politics' is not simply a question of the attitudes taken by those people who happen to be aged under thirty-five. Young people are leading the demand for a politics of the future, rejecting the current political and economic consensus as not only unfair but also unsustainable. In Britain, this may well continue to take the form of a re-engagement with the political life of the nations and regions, given that the Westminster establishment has otherwise proved disastrously resistant to change.

Conclusion

Growing up under a particular kind of neoliberal globalisation does not mean that under thirty-fives conform to this way of thinking and being. Constructing identities through consumption of global culture, lifestyle choices, sexual orientations and trans-national political movements, may imply that younger demographics have turned their back on all forms of collective solidarity rooted in place or national democracy. But this is only a pragmatic reaction to a political and social landscape where the nation-state's power has weakened. It does not mean that the politics of nationhood has become irrelevant. There is now a vacuum, which many different forces, parties and movements are rushing to fill.

Younger demographics in Britain have so far approached the nation on democratic lines. In Scotland, young people have pushed hard to rejuvenate civil society and democracy in their nation, seeking independence in order to ensure greater solidarity with those living in Scotland and beyond its borders, through a return to the moral compass of social democracy and moving against aggressive foreign policy. The referendum in September 2014 led many young people to recognise their shared interests with migrants and the economically disadvantaged of all ages, whether or not they were aware of this in the framework of 'precarity' or of a 'precarious' class. UKIP approaches the nation on ethnic lines, and addresses the anxiety of an uncertain future by finding scapegoats to blame. The party has thus far not come near the youth vote, despite rising disaffection, disadvantage and resentment amongst younger demographics following the implementation of austerity.

We only need to look across the waters to Europe to see that we can't take this dynamic within Britain for granted. Independence movements that attract young people as supporters and leaders are not necessarily as clear-sighted and inclusive in their approach as the Scottish 'Yes' movement. In fact, it may turn out to have been an exceptional moment. Europe is heading into dangerously unpredictable times. The majority of young people who don't exercise their vote at the ballot box want real change – not the 'switcheroo' of political parties but new forces and movements, constitutional alignments and new states. At the time of writing, Catalonia looks likely to hold an unofficial referendum on independence, again led by young people who have borne the brunt of austerity in Spain, with a 55 per cent youth unemployment rate. Independence movements have emerged or are gaining ground in the Basque country and Venetia in Italy, as well as in Ukraine, to mention some of the most notable. Young people's precarity, under- and un-employment and uncertain future leave us vulnerable to the appeal of the far right and arguments for a 'return to the nation' based on ethnic, rather than democratic lines.

Finally, my generation faces immense challenges that require international co-operation on an unprecedented scale. How we are able to confront these will in part depend on our relationship to the nation-state, whose role is in transition. The Scottish independence referendum showed that, where demands for democratic revival and constitutional change are met with a genuine outlet for expression, young people respond with peaceful, wide-scale and transformative engagement. In Britain, the weakness and instability of the Union, and the detachment of younger demographics from the 'British' identity, should not mean that we ignore or dismiss the politics of nationhood. This will be crucial in how we respond to and influence the volatile politics that is set to reshape Britain and Europe, even if our ultimate aim is a borderless world.

Niki Seth-Smith is Co-Founder of Precarious Europe, a media project on young people and the 'new politics' in Europe.

Breaking the first rule of generation Y

Adam Ramsay

In 2010, the combined membership of the Green Parties in the UK was around 10,000. Now, it sits at more than 63,000. This is an astonishing level of growth, for three reasons.

Firstly, conventional wisdom teaches that Greens do badly when Labour are in opposition. Secondly, political party membership in general is in decline. Thirdly, a vast proportion of this membership is under the age of thirty. Specifically, between January 2014 and December 2014, the number of signed up Young Greens multiplied by more than five.

Thousands of people broke the first rule of generation Y: don't join anything.

It's not just the Greens. After the referendum in Scotland, the Scottish National Party saw a huge rise in its membership. It now stands at more than 92,000. Given that the average age of the 134,000 UK Conservative members is said to be sixty-eight, and considering how many young people got involved in the Yes campaign in Scotland, it seems likely that the Scottish National Party now has more members under thirty than the UK Conservative Party does. Membership of Plaid Cymru is also up and, by all accounts, their youth membership is from the radical left of the party.

None of this surprises me as much as one simple moment. On the last day of the Occupy Democracy protests in Parliament Square, I was asked to speak. In the question and answer session afterwards, I posed a problem: if someone wants to get involved in radical politics in their area, where do they go? What do they do? How do they find other people to organise with? And I suggested a solution: people should join the Green Party. I assumed this would be hugely controversial. I expected to be shouted down. Instead, this heresy was greeted with jazz hands of agreement from a good number of people.

All of this comes as something of a shock. Just a few years ago – a few months ago – the story of British politics was that parties were dead. Young people in particular, we were told, would never join; the future belonged to 38 Degrees, Avaaz and disparate, fleeting, horizontalist groups set up around specific actions and events. But then, the way that we organise has been transforming rapidly in recent years, and perhaps this is the logical conclusion of that process. Or, at least, the next step.

To explain, let's go back to the year I was born. On 3 March 1985, the miners' strike ended and, symbolically at least, the power of trade unions in Britain was broken. On 10 July that same year, Greenpeace's ship 'Rainbow Warrior' was sunk by the French secret service in New Zealand, capturing global headlines and generating a flood of members for the organisation. I've sometimes thought that that summer marked the symbolic hand over from one form of radical politics to another.

Greenpeace was founded in the 1960s – as were a string of other organisations, including Amnesty International, Friends of the Earth, the World Development Movement (well, 1970), and Third World First (now People & Planet). Together, these groups represent a particular cross-section of civil society – asking radical questions about specific global issues, building mass membership databases nationally and internationally, and encouraging people to organise not for their own rights, but for those of others. They are long term organisations rather than specific, short term protests. In a sense, these were legacy institutions of the environmental, peace, equalities and human rights social movements that emerged in the 1960s and 1970s.

There is an argument that the growth in these NGOs was a product of technological development – with changes in banks allowing standing orders to be set up more easily, and reforms in postal systems making it simpler to send out mass mailings. But there's another way to see their rise: these groups provided organising platforms and a voice for the generation of baby boomers who had gone through the 1960s expansion of higher education. They offered an outlet for progressive politics for people who identified beyond class struggle (or who saw themselves as newly middle class), who benefitted from the stability of the welfare state and who were interested in campaigning on issues beyond their own or their immediate community's material circumstances.

If, like me, you were born that summer, between the miners' strike ending, and the Rainbow Warrior sinking, then Baghdad was bombed in your last few months of sixth form. For pretty much everyone who was politically active in my time at university, this was what first got them involved. And, afterwards, there was plenty to keep us active. In 2005, the G8 came to the UK – with its following carnival of anarchic resistance. This was still (just) the era of the summit-hopping anti-globalisation movement, and thousands from across the UK came to Edinburgh to protest against this gathering of the world's most powerful men.

Many left with a sense that the big NGO 'Make Poverty History' campaign had sold them out when it declared flimsy proposals announced at the summit to be a victory, and much of the activist left of my generation moved towards anarchism. Hot on the heels of the G8, climate change took centre stage. Thousands mobilised for a string of annual protests, for community action, for widespread civil disobedience. People demanded carbon reduction targets, questioned the role of banks in driving the crisis, got naked, and glued themselves to the icons of the capitalist system they held responsible – both to shut them down and to get on the front pages.

But one of the things that is notable about my generation, the Iraq War generation, is how few of us became active in the NGOs our parents had built, despite the fact that they were often the groups who had educated us on these issues in the first place. Of scores of environmental activists I know of about my age, I can only think of one who became a long-term Friends of the Earth group member. Instead, people set up their own, new organisations. For environmentalists, there was The Camp for Climate Action, and, now, Reclaim the Power. For those – ever more after the banks collapsed in 2008 – campaigning around the global economy, very few seem to go to regular local Global Justice Now (the renamed World Development Movement) meetings. These seem largely to have remained the preserve of the generation who founded them.

Some of this is about the sorts of activism in vogue: it's very difficult for an organisation with staff to support campaigners to do anything illegal. Even Greenpeace only allow very limited numbers, in very controlled circumstances, to break the law. Some of it is about our changed economy: it's difficult to go to a consistent Wednesday night meeting if you do shift work in a cafe, or have to move house and area every few months. Organisational models designed for the stability of mid-twentieth-century social democracy don't necessarily function for twenty-first-century precarity.

Part of it is about the internet. One function of a central office used to be to disseminate carefully researched briefings nationally, by sending letters to local organisers to be read out at their next meeting. I can now do the same thing in two seconds by posting a link to a Wikipedia page on the wall of a Facebook group. Partly, it's about the right tool for the right job – sometimes, it probably does make sense to build a temporary organisation for a specific task, rather than joining something longer term. But I can't help but feel that the general refusal of Thatcher's children to join anything more permanent is about something else too: a reflection of an individualised and throw-away culture, of people too atomised to be willing to sign up to any group.

The main reason I've been given by people who basically share the politics of the Green Party for not joining it is that they value their independence. They don't want to be tied into something. They don't want to lose their sense of autonomy. There's another way of putting this: they are too much of an individualist to join a collective. They don't want to be associated with someone else, and to have to take some of the blame when that other person does or says something stupid. Deep down, my suspicion is that that psychology is part of the reason we don't go to our local Global Justice Now meetings either. Thatcher once said that her object was to change our souls. She did.

In a sense, there's something ironic in all of this. These explanations of the refusal to join anything often come with a hint of the rhetoric of anarchist moral authority. But in practice, lots of anarchists are willing to join groups and organise as long-term collectives. Some even have their own organisations somewhat akin to political parties – notably SolFed and AFed.

Likewise, I can't help thinking that this refusal of my generation to join anything is a huge problem. Because I've still never had a better answer to my question: if someone wants to get involved in radical politics in your area, where do they go? Instead, much of the activist left lives and takes political action in small cliques. New comrades are largely only attracted through occasional mass protest camps or as refugees from groups like the Socialist Workers' Party, whose ruthless centralised structure allows them to organise frequent recruitment drives but has also festered a culture of grotesque rape-apologism and cynical undermining of other left groups.

Almost as significantly, all-too-often fictitious non-hierarchy, in practice, just means that the media appoints spokespeople. And all too often, the people chosen by the press aren't those the movements would have voted for, and are those who fit neatly into the conventional mould of 'leader' in a sexist, classist, racist society. Contrast this with the nine leaders, co-leaders or deputies of the Green Parties of the four nations of the UK – only two of whom are straight, white men.

Perhaps the main reason people haven't joined anything, is that every institution our forebears left for us has failed or is failing. The Labour party has utterly capitulated to global capital. Since the foundation of the NGOs of the 1960s, neoliberalism has taken over the world, the environmental crisis has become entrenched, global inequality has soared and war and human rights abuses have continued. Modern unions have presided over an historic erosion of wages and workers' rights and the Green Party has, so far, delivered only one MP. It's no wonder we have so little faith in organisations.

Or we did. Because the mass influx of members to the Greens and to the SNP implies that something has changed. And the fact that, in part, this was a product of the Scottish referendum is in itself telling. After the vote, English radicals would often ask the question: what can we learn from the Yes movement in Scotland? An obvious response to that was: 'what did the Yes movement itself learn?' One answer is that tens of thousands went through the most engaging political debate in Britain in a generation, and came to the conclusion that something as old fashioned as a political party can be relevant in the modern world after all.

I think this tells us a few things about what some might call 'the youth of today'. The first is that single issue campaigns are no longer enough. It's becoming increasingly clear that we don't live in a world where things are basically fine, except for needing the odd tweak. Instead we live in a world that's utterly fucked, and people are starting to see that the problem is not a shopping list of isolated issues, but an interconnected system which is failing the vast majority of people. That means we need organisations which will allow us to join with others and take action on one issue today, and another tomorrow, without having to pretend that there is no connection between them.

Secondly, the fact that our generation is used to speaking for ourselves does not seem to preclude having someone else speaking for us too – at least to some extent. People are willing to build a bigger platform together and give a spokesperson a leg up onto it. Usually, our social movements have spokespeople appointed for them by the press, and activists spend a lot of time criticising whoever the appointed one happens to be this week. But because the Green Party elects its leaders and representatives, people seem more content to allow them to get on with it.

Thirdly, in an era of social media, there is still some value in long term organisations. There is a simple way to put this: the Green Party of England and Wales has 150,000 Facebook followers. It takes time to build up that following just as it did in the past to build up a mailing list. Facebook groups, in which members discuss news stories, debate policy and create memes have become institutions in the party, but they too took time to build.

Finally, there are lots on the left who have retreated from electoralism in the past. I think it's important not to fetishise a cross in a box every few years, but I also think it's vital not to ignore it as one tactic among many.

There is, perhaps, another way to see all this. I came into politics at the tail end of the anti-globalisation movement. As a young Green member in the early and mid 2000s, I was a bit weird. As my thirtieth birthday looms into sight, there seems now to be a younger generation, who were mobilised by the 2010 anti-austerity protests. They have very different attitudes to politics than people my age did when we were their age, and their experiences have taught them different lessons. I confess, I find their approach to organising gives me much more hope.

Adam Ramsay is Co-Editor of the UK section of openDemocracy, co-founder of bright-green.org, author of *42 Reasons to Support Scottish Independence* and the Green Party's European election manifesto. He previously worked for student activist network People & Planet and once upon a time was student president at Edinburgh University.

What would a better democracy look like?

Sarah Allan

If you're expecting a chapter on how to increase voter turnout and send membership of political parties soaring, then I am going to disappoint.

Our democracy is broken precisely because the ways it offers us to engage are so outdated. We can vote for a party, join a party, stand for office as a party candidate. But is it surprising that we don't when only 36 per cent of us have a 'very' or 'fairly' strong attachment to a party?[3]

I'm not denying that voting is important – it is. Efforts to make voting easier are worthwhile. It is an outrage that in modern society, disabled people still often struggle to use and access polling stations.[2] It shouldn't happen that people are stopped from voting by confusing registration forms.[3]

But all too often this is where ideas for a better democracy stop. And here lies the problem. People aren't usually turned off from politics because of what happens on election day itself. They don't decide not to join a party because of events in one twenty four hour period every few years. It's what happens *between* elections that is so out of step with our lives and expectations.

And this is what needs to change.

What's wrong with UK 'democracy'?

A system view

Our political system is based on the idea of representative democracy. This suggests that society is too large and political decisions too complex for us to take them ourselves. Instead we elect politicians to represent us in making these decisions. In theory, elections make politicians' actions legitimate. They allow us to choose between parties' policy manifestos – manifestos which tell us what they will do in government. They are supposed to enable us to hold politicians to account: we can vote them out if we're unhappy with what they do.

In practice this system is no longer working, if it ever did.

Firstly, the extent to which the system is providing *legitimacy and accountability* is highly questionable. Turnouts are low and gaps in turnout between different groups have widened. In 1987, turnout amongst the poorest income group was only 4 per cent lower than turnout amongst the wealthiest. By 2010, the difference was 23 per cent. The gap in turnout between eighteen to twenty-four year olds and those aged over sixty-five has almost doubled, from 18 per cent in 1970 to 32 per cent in 2010.[4] Politicians are evidently not legitimised by, or accountable to, all sections of society.

Even if everyone did vote, governments pass many policies that were not included in their party manifestos. Key decisions are also not always made by politicians. In 2011, for example, the government introduced Local Enterprise Partnerships (LEPs). LEPs are bodies made up of local businesses and local councils, and are business-led. They decide local priorities for investment in roads, buildings and facilities.[5] They also play a major role in decisions about how to create local jobs and economic growth.[6] Yet the vast majority of LEP members are not elected; the public do not choose them and cannot get rid of them.

Just as legitimacy and accountability are an issue, so is *representation*. Elections are a foregone conclusion in many parts of the country. Bootle in Merseyside has elected a Labour MP at every election since 1945. Beckenham in Bromley has had a Conservative MP since 1950. Political parties therefore focus their attention away from these areas. They concentrate on seats that are closely fought. More specifically, they concentrate on the people in those seats who are likely to vote but haven't yet decided who to vote for.[7] This has an impact on parties' policies.

Firstly, there is a worrying overlap between groups that are less likely to vote and those being most disadvantaged by policy decisions. For example, non-voters in the 2010 general election faced cuts worth 20 per cent of their household budget in that year's spending review. The equivalent figure for those who did vote was 12 per cent.[8] Secondly, parties' focus on the same areas and voters means that different parties' policies have become more similar . Because the electoral system makes it harder for small parties to win seats, voters are left with a much narrower choice of potential prime ministers and governments.

Decision-makers' genders, ethnicities and educational backgrounds also challenge the idea that politicians are representative. There are more male MPs in Parliament today than there have been women MPs since 1945. More than one third of MPs elected in 2010 attended fee paying schools (including twenty who went to Eton), compared with less than 10 per cent of the adult national population.[9]

The current system has also proved inadequate for dealing with long-term issues like climate change. This has a strong effect on generational representation: young people both tend to care about these issues more and are most likely to be impacted by them. Representative democracy claims to work better than direct citizen involvement, but does it?

What's changed?

UK society is radically different to when representative democracy was introduced.[10] New technologies connect us with each other across time and geographical space. We are also better-educated, and have access to a much greater range of information. These changes challenge the rationale that society is too large and issues are too complex for people to play a direct role in decision-making. This makes the current system's failings less acceptable. Manifestos have never given us a say on every key decision, but this problem is now fixable; people could easily play a role in decision-making between elections. The fact that this is rare – and where it happens often poorly undertaken – only breeds further disconnection from a system that seems far behind the times.

Today the UK public is also less likely to support a particular political party. This is true of all age groups, but the figures for young people are the most stark. In 2012, only 66 per cent of British people in their twenties and early thirties identified with a party, compared to 85 per cent of the same age group in 1983. Even where it exists, our support for parties is less strong. Just 36 per cent of today's British public say they have a 'very strong' or 'fairly strong' attachment to a party.[11]

One reason for this fall in partisanship is likely to be parties' increased similarity – both in terms of policies and in their personnel, language and communication styles.[12] It has become easier to see politicians as an elite who have more in common with each other than with us – the people they are meant to represent.[13]

Despite this, the main way we are asked to engage is still by voting for a party. Perhaps it is unsurprising that many young people feel disengaged from mainstream politics.

Deliberative democracy

A new version of democracy must offer people real chances to influence, and be involved in, decision-making between elections. 'Deliberative' techniques are a key way to achieve this. These are methods which involve people sharing their views, knowledge and experiences.

The participatory budgeting model developed in Porto Alegre, Brasil, is a famous example. Now used in over 1500 cities, towns and local areas worldwide,[14] this gives the public a powerful role in deciding how to spend local budgets. At its most basic, it starts with neighbourhood assemblies that are open to all residents. Residents discuss local needs and draw up a list of desired spending. They also elect two representatives. One then works with decision-makers (and representatives from other neighbourhoods) to shape the budget. The other acts as a channel of communication between this process and their local area; they also supervise the budget's implementation.[15]

Analysis of participatory budgeting across Brazil found that it resulted in spending which better reflected public priorities. As these priorities were sanitation and healthcare, it also led to a substantial decrease in infant deaths.[16]

In the UK, participatory budgeting has mainly only been tried at a local level and with small amounts of money. It usually involves inviting everyone in the area to an event where they discuss and vote on spending options. Popular spending choices have included play and sports facilities, activities for young people and health initiatives. A government evaluation of projects in Manton, Newcastle, Stockport, Southampton and Tower Hamlets found they had had a significant impact despite their small scale. This included additional funding for deprived areas, changes in the types of projects receiving funding and increased confidence amongst participants in tackling local issues. In areas where it was a specific aim, the number of people voting in elections also increased. In Worksop South East, the council ward in which Manton is based, it rose from 22 per cent to 51 per cent.[17]

Whilst participatory budgeting is about overall priorities, deliberative techniques can also be used in specific policy areas. In 2002 Nottinghamshire Healthcare NHS Trust ran a deliberative event to help it improve local health services. It used a method called 'Open Space' which gives participants control of the agenda: attendees decided which topics should be discussed by compiling a list of their biggest concerns. The 120 people who took part - including service users, carers and health staff – suggested introducing assisted transport and establishing a new users' and carers' resource centre, among other recommendations.[18] The Trust introduced these changes.

Given the huge range of deliberative and participatory techniques available,[19] it is possible for decision-makers in all policy areas and at all levels – local, national and international – to involve the public in key decisions. This should be a central, vital part of our democracy.

Who participates?

In an improved democracy, no group's needs would be systematically overlooked, and all sections of society would take part. One part of the solution is to offer more alienated or marginalised groups specially tailored ways to get involved. Decision-makers should work with communities to design and decide on these opportunities to make sure they are effective.

Decision-makers should also do more to tackle resource inequality. People's time, money, health and access to transport can all affect how likely they are to participate. The same is true of education, confidence and personal networks.[20] Of course, combating socio-economic inequality would involve comprehensive, structural political overhaul, but an important part of this is enabling and increasing political participation with tailored support for people to get involved. Two organisations that are experts in this area are Bite the Ballot and the SHM Foundation.

Bite the Ballot engages with young people, encouraging them to vote. A core part of its work involves members of the organisation going into schools and talking with young people about the issues that are important to them, broadening to a participatory discussion about how voting can impact on these areas. At the end of the lesson pupils can choose to fill out a voter registration form – usually everyone does. Bite the Ballot also undertakes a huge amount of activity online, including on YouTube. It recently ran 'Leaders Live', a series of live online events which gave young people the chance to question each party leader in turn in the run-up to this May's general election.

The SHM Foundation works with young people to make their voices heard and develop a new generation of leaders. Their project 'LOOP' empowers young people to improve schools and colleges. SHM Foundation members train student leaders at each school to design and run workshops. The students then hold events for their peers in individual course areas, creating reviews which are published on the LOOP website.[21] The site is publicly available; prospective students and parents can use it to decide which schools and courses to choose. At the end of the school year, the SHM Foundation brings together key staff and a cross section of students at each institution. They discuss and decide what changes need to be made, giving young people a much-needed positive early experience of participation.

Bite the Ballot's and the SHM Foundation's work have a number of features in common. They involve going to where young people are already (both online and offline) and using language which is relevant to us. They are founded on an understanding of our motivations and help us to acquire the skills and knowledge to take part. A new version of democracy should put a greater emphasis on engagement – on thinking about how to reach groups currently less likely to participate.

Conclusion

A vote every five years isn't good enough. Though politicians do occasionally suggest democratic reforms, their ideas are too often focused on introducing more elected representatives and shifting power between levels of decision-makers. This does nothing to create genuine political transformation.

Our political system needs a fundamental rebalancing – away from representation and towards participation. A more participatory democracy would make our politics more legitimate, accountable and representative. If politics felt more relevant to our everyday lives, then perhaps young people would see more point in taking part.

Sarah Allan is Democratic Reform Lead at Involve. She believes passionately in the need to create a democracy where people are able to take and influence the decisions that affect their lives. Involve works to inspire, innovate and embed change that achieves just that.

Notes

1. British Social Attitudes survey, 'A disengaged Britain? Political interest and participation over 30 years', 2013. http://bsa-30.natcen.ac.uk/read-the-report/politics/introduction.aspx
2. Clive Gilbert, Christina Sarb, and Marc Bush, 'Polls apart 2010: Opening elections to disabled people', Scope, 2010. http://www.scope.org.uk/Scope/media/Documents/Publication%20Directory/Polls-apart-2010.pdf?ext=.pdf
3. Alex Andreou and Shiv Malik, 'EU citizens stopped from voting in UK after confusion over registration forms', *The Guardian*, 24 May 2014. http://www.theguardian.com/politics/2014/may/24/eu-citizens-prevented-voting-confusion-registration-forms
4. Sarah Birch, Glenn Gottfried and Guy Lodge, 'Divided Democracy: Political inequality in the UK and why it matters', IPPR, 2013.
5. 'Supporting economic growth through local enterprise partnerships and enterprise zones', Gov.uk, 7 November 2012. https://www.gov.uk/government/policies/supporting-economic-growth-through-local-enterprise-partnerships-and-enterprise-zones/supporting-pages/local-enterprise-partnerships
6. http://www.lepnetwork.net/
7. Chris Terry's 'Penny for your vote?' report for the Electoral Reform Society demonstrates this, by looking at how much parties spend during election campaigns in different areas. http://www.electoral-reform.org.uk/images/dynamicImages/file/ERS_Penny%20for%20your%20vote_Final.pdf
8. Sarah Birch, Glenn Gottfried and Guy Lodge, 'Divided Democracy: Political inequality in the UK and why it matters', IPPR, 2013.
9. 'Characteristics of the new House of Commons', Parliament.uk, 2010. http://www.parliament.uk/business/publications/research/key-issues-for-the-new-parliament/the-new-parliament/characteristics-of-the-new-house-of-commons/
10. This section doesn't cover every change in this period. Instead it picks out two key examples. Other important and recent differences include the rise of twenty-four-hour news coverage, trends towards so-called 'open government' including greater public access to government data, and the Equalities Acts of recent decades which have made it illegal to discriminate on grounds such as age, race and sexual orientation.
11. British Social Attitudes survey, 'A disengaged Britain? Political interest and participation over thirty years', British Social Attitudes 30, 2013. http://bsa-30.natcen.ac.uk/read-the-report/politics/introduction.aspx

12. These latter changes are often described as part of the 'professionalisation' of politics and political communication. The points on language and style are often associated with changes in the media, such as the rise of twenty-four-hour news coverage.

13. Some other possible causes of declining partisanship are discussed in British Social Attitudes survey, 'The role of class in shaping social attitudes', British Social Attitudes 30, 2013. http://bsa-30.natcen.ac.uk/read-the-report/social-class/introduction.aspx

14. Diether W. Beuermann, and Maria Amelina, 'Does Participatory Budgeting Improve Decentralized Public Service Delivery?' IDB Working Paper Series No. IDB-WP-547, November 2014.

15. Sónia Gonçalves, 'Power to the People: The Effects of Participatory Budgeting on Municipal Expenditures and Infant Mortality in Brazil', Job Market Paper. http://www.webmeets.com/files/papers/LACEA-LAMES/2009/714/Sonia%20Goncalves.pdf

16. *Ibid.*

17. SQW, Cambridge Economic Associates, Geoff Fordham Associates, 'Communities in the driving seat: a study of Participatory Budgeting in England', DCLG, 2011.

18. 'People and participation', Involve, 2005. http://www.involve.org.uk//wp-content/uploads/2011/03/People-and-Participation.pdf

19. To find out about more techniques see, for example: the second half of Involve's 'People and participation' (for a wide range of deliberative methods and UK case studies); Thiago Peixoto's excellent http://democracyspot.net/ (for the latest international examples and research) and Laura Black's article 'The Promise and Problems of online deliberation' (for online examples). It's also worth noting that deliberative techniques are not always the answer. For example, a referendum was definitely the right way for Scotland to decide on independence as it provided a simple way for everyone in the country to take part. Where deliberative techniques might have been useful here was in letting the Scottish people decide what question they should be asked in the referendum. Countries like Switzerland use referenda frequently http://www.swissworld.org/en/politics/peoples_rights/peoples_rights/. Finally, although this author disagrees, some people favour removing elected representatives altogether. See for example http://www.andrewbadr.com/log/24/delegative-democracy-a-scalable-voting-model/

20. Ellie Brodie, Tim Hughes, Véronique Jochum, Sarah Miller, Nick Ockenden, Diane Warburton, 'Pathways through participation: what creates and sustains active citizenship', 2011.

21. http://loop.uk.com/

What the frack? Resurgent environmentalism in the UK

Robbie Gillett

A group of women from Blackpool are hurrying towards a farm gate with chains in their hands. 'It's just a bit nerve-wracking because none of us have done this before', they explain. It's 5am. Dressed in traditional Lancashire headscarves and bright yellow tabards, the women successfully squat a field where fracking firm Cuadrilla Resources have plans to drill for shale gas. For most of the group, which calls itself 'Operation Mothers and Grandmas' (#OMG), it is their first experience of direct action. As unconventional oil and gas companies have attempted to establish a foothold in the UK in the last five years, many communities now find themselves on the frontline against these new extractive industries. A broad new wave of environmental justice is emerging to fight back, embedded within a wider anti-austerity and social justice framework.

These new groups are different from climate campaigns of the late 2000s. As the bankers' bail out and austerity measures transformed the political landscape after 2010, many activists who had developed their organising skills through climate campaigning, turned their efforts to fighting the government's neoliberal attacks: notably the trebling of tuition fees, plans to privatise the NHS, workfare, the bedroom tax and the criminalisation of squatting. In 2011, at the same time as slashing public services and letting tax dodgers off the hook, Chancellor George Osborne announced: 'We're not going to save the planet by putting our country out of business'.[1] With multi-pronged attacks being implemented in the short-term, a continued focus on the longer-term threat of climate change in the midst of the dismantling of the welfare state didn't feel tenable. In the mainstream, discussions on climate justice received dwindling attention – especially following the failed United Nations talks in Copenhagen in 2009.

Consequently, there has been a keen desire to re-connect environmentalism with our everyday lives – and to better articulate the connections between capitalism, poverty and environmental destruction. Groups such as Fuel Poverty Action, formed in 2011, exemplify this approach well. Each winter people face soaring heating bills and poorly insulated houses. At weekday coffee mornings in church halls and community centres, pensioners discuss blockading 'Big Six' energy firms and government departments.[2] By linking rising rents and caps to housing benefit with demands for an affordable, clean energy system, it becomes possible to highlight how environmental justice can and should be embedded within social struggles.

Similarly, whilst newer activist groups like UK Uncut do not primarily address climate change, it still forms part of their wider analysis of the role of profiteering corporations and finance capitalism in undermining our collective futures. Some of the instigators of these groups learned direct action and consensus decision-making partly through the Climate Camp network which ran from 2006 to 2011. These action camps were set up in opposition to proposed new carbon-intensive infrastructure projects, such as a third runway at Heathrow Airport and a new coal-fired power station at Kingsnorth in Kent. These have both been shelved for the time being. With austerity kicking in from 2010, climate activists were able to contribute both their action skills and anti-capitalist ethos to these new networks.

Fracked Off

But, quietly at first, in the midst of this climate hiatus from 2010 onwards, a new threat to communities across the UK emerged out of the nascent 'extreme energy' industry. Hydraulic fracturing, or 'fracking', involves blasting high volumes of water and chemicals into drilled wells to force open cracks in the rock formation, allowing escaping gas to be tapped. The industry has already left a toxic legacy in the United States and parts of Australia; these consequences have been well-documented, including water contamination from the chemicals used, air pollution and dangerous health effects.[3] While the number of exploratory wells in the UK may be limited at present, commercial production at profitable rates will requires thousands of well pads across the countryside, as well as heavy truck movements and pipelines. Plans to frack up to 60 per cent of the English countryside have catalysed environmental concerns outside of the usual interested constituencies. And beyond these immediate effects, desperately squeezing out the last of the difficult-to-reach fossils fuels does nothing to halt our rising carbon emissions. As Julian Huppert MP stated to an anti-fracking protest outside Parliament in January 2015: 'Scrabbling around for the fag ends of fossil fuels is not the answer'.

This threat, however, also presents an opportunity for communities to mobilise not just in opposition to fracking, but around issues of energy justice and community control. The relatively small 'Frack Off' organisation, along with Friends of the Earth, have supported the emergence of over 160 residents' groups fighting extreme energy plans in towns and villages across the UK and Ireland over the last five years. This has involved the slow and patient work of awareness-raising, relationship-building, legal support and training. Though this might not grab newspaper headlines, it has been crucial to building up a key strand of opposition to the fracking industry. Since it is local communities who may be forced to live with new fracking sites, it is these same communities who are best placed to anchor the long-term resistance that will be needed to make the industry unworkable. Moratoriums in France, Germany and the state of New York, backed by social movements, have provided useful encouragement and precedents for the UK. UK groups have also drawn inspiration from the 'Lock the Gate' tactics in Australia, where farmers and communities have successfully halted the arrival of fracking firms by literally locking field gates, mobilising *en masse* and removing the 'social licence' for companies to operate.[4]

These two approaches, moratoriums and community resistance, highlight different political dynamics in stopping extreme energy industries. Moratoriums can provide useful interim measures. After early fracking operations by Cuadrilla Resources caused an earthquake in Blackpool in 2010, the UK government imposed a temporary twelve month ban. More recently, in January 2015, the Scottish government introduced a temporary halt on the granting of new planning consents. But such approaches risk being over-turned in the future. On the other hand, deep-rooted and widespread community opposition can make it difficult or impossible for fracking firms to operate regardless of the changing positions of successive governments. The financial costs to firms in fighting legal challenges and providing security for sites can eat into already squeezed profit margins. Tellingly, the coalition has announced its intention to restrict the use of judicial reviews by campaigning organisations or individuals. Although such legal methods can be prohibitively expensive for activists, in favourable circumstances they can still be used to overturn planning decisions and challenge government policy.

Balcombe, Barton Moss and the Community Protection Camps

In July 2013 Cuadrilla Resources began exploratory drilling at a site in Balcombe in Sussex, located between two major activist bases of Brighton and London. The company were met by vexed local residents, 82 per cent of whom were opposed to the company's plans.[5] A colourful and vibrant roadside protest camp was hastily set up with activists from the surrounding area, providing daily resistance to the company's operations. Later in the year, a similar camp would be set up in Barton Moss in Salford where the company Igas conducted exploratory drilling for four months. As community resistance, these camps form a second key strand to the anti-fracking movement, along with opposition from residents' groups.

The 'Community Protection Camps', as they are referred to by those living there, have provided a logistical headache for fracking firms and the police forces doing their bidding. Each drill site requires dozens of truck movements each week. These were delayed by protectors walking slowly in front of vehicles, using lock-on devices in the road and climbing on top of trucks. Police responses were heavy-handed. Of the 114 charges brought against ninety individuals for the Balcombe protests in summer of 2013, only twenty-nine resulted in convictions.[6] Activists engaged in symbolic and creative blockades: using an old fire engine to block the entrance at the Balcombe site and leaving a fifty-six foot wind turbine blade across the gates at Barton Moss. Other camps have now emerged at Upton in Chester, West Newton in East Yorkshire (disbanded), Crawberry Hill (evicted January 2015), Borras near Wrexham and Horsehill in Surrey. Sympathetic local residents keep these camps well-stocked with supplies of food, firewood and blankets. Trade unions such as Unite and the Public and Commercial Services union have also passed policy to support anti-fracking camps, as well as opposing fracking nationally.[7]

A strong DIY ethos underpins these sites, with a focus on action, rather than process. I was involved in the Barton Moss camp in Salford, where camp participants used a competing mix of approaches. Some were unwilling to hold formal meetings: their 'just-get-on-with it' approach won out due to the urgencies of camp maintenance during a harsh winter, vehicle blockading and arrestee support. Measured by their *outcomes*, such as truck delays, community involvement and press coverage – the camps have been a great success. But measured by the *process* with which these outcomes were achieved, the camps have not always nurtured the prefigurative politics of democratic decision-making or inter-personal conflict resolution.

Nonetheless, exploratory drilling by companies such as Cuadrilla and Igas are not only conducted with the sole purpose of examining the geology of underground rock formations. They are also measuring the level of community resistance. As one observer at a shale industry conference, who wished to remain anonymous, noted: 'Every truck that is blockaded; every planning application that is mired in bureaucracy: it's killing the industry'. The combined resistance of residents' groups, protector camps and legal manoeuvres by NGOs has already put a brake on the industry establishing itself, despite David Cameron's willingness to go 'all out' for shale gas.

'Reclaim the Power', a national network aiming to mobilise around economic, social and environmental justice, has played a part in this resistance. Germinated by a group using the name 'No Dash for Gas' – who occupied a gas-fired power station for seven days in 2012, the network's main output has been to organise temporary, squatted, mass action camps to skill up new people in direct action.[8] In doing so, we provide an entry point for getting involved in radical politics of solidarity, action-planning and consensus decision making – in a similar way that the Climate Camps provided a formative experience for a whole generation of anti-authoritarian activists. These larger camps are different from the semi-permanent roadside protection camps and act as an engagement point for people who cannot (or prefer not) to live full time on the handful of anti-fracking camps dotted around the country. When not organising camps, the network is made up of regional groups, largely based in cities, who can organise and take action together closer to home.

Following the announcement that Reclaim the Power would hold its first camp at Balcombe in August 2013, Cuadrilla Resources responded by closing the drilling site for the six day duration of the event. Around 2000 people attended a 'Solidarity Sunday' with coaches arriving from around the country. The following day of action saw company headquarters and PR firms blockaded as well as the arrest of Green MP Caroline Lucas outside the Balcombe site gates.

The following summer of 2014, with an enlarged network, Reclaim the Power responded to Blackpool residents who are fighting Cuadrilla's new plans for a commercial fracking site at Preston New Road. As our relationships with residents' groups have deepened, tactics begin to overlap. 'Operation Mothers and Grandmas' took and held their squatted field for one week before Reclaim the Power activists arrived with marquees, kitchens and compost loos ready for a week-long action camp. Our two groups went on to take joint action together, including the occupation of Cuadrilla's office and actions against the local Council, fracking research institutions, government departments and drilling sites.

What impact has this growing movement had so far? The resistance at Balcombe has been identified as a clear turning point in public attitudes towards fracking. Research by the University of Nottingham showed that previously rising support for fracking began to reverse following the Balcombe protests, with a highpoint of 58.3 per cent in July 2013 (before the protests) falling to 54 per cent in September 2013 (after). This new downward trend continued during subsequent protests at Barton Moss - with public support for fracking dropping to 49.7 per cent in May 2014.[9]

The Green Surge

What does all this mean for young people today? No particular age group is over-represented in the anti-fracking movement – it is a healthy cross-generational mix. Within this however, are many for whom visiting an anti-fracking camp or event has been their first experience of being politically active beyond the ballot box. For the first time in a generation though, interest in party politics is cautiously returning.[10] While distrust and disinterest in electoral politics has been a dominant view amongst the horizontalist left for over twenty years, this tendency is beginning to shift with the crumbling of support for the three centrist parties and with UKIP dragging the political spectrum to the right. Within this context, the Green Party stand as the only sizeable and genuinely left-wing party willing to fight austerity and the climate crisis together. Still, if the Greens are to have any kind of influence on a minority government, social movements who are supporting them will need to remain vigilant and mobilised.

Internationally, there has been renewed attention given to securing a global climate deal, as well as to financial divestment campaigns against public institutions with investments in oil and gas companies.[11] 400,000 people attended the People's Climate March in New York in September 2014 ahead of the UN climate talks, with 40,000 marching in London on the same day. The New York event was characterised by the involvement of shorefront communities who had been battered by Hurricane Sandy in 2012, as well as Pennsylvanian communities left with the toxic impact of around 90,000 fracking wells. This re-articulated the climate debate in a manner similar to Fuel Poverty Action in the UK, demonstrating that environmental degradation is hitting us in the here and now, as well as threatening our long term future. Situating environmental concerns within a wider left framework of social inequality and corporate dominance remains key.

European direct action and NGO networks are currently gearing up for the UN climate talks in Paris in December 2015. Whether people will be able to travel to Paris *en masse*, with an expectation that any negotiated deal will likely be inadequate – and still return with momentum to fight our battles at home is yet to be seen. Can taking action together with other global networks create something bigger than the sum of our parts? Will it create inspiration and hope for an alternative collective future? The ghost of the failed international climate talks in Copenhagen in 2009 and the subsequent loss of momentum in this area continues to stalk these conversations. As neoliberalism staggers on, wounded but not defeated, environmental justice movements will need to form part of a resurgent and multi-faceted left that is both unafraid to confront corporate interests and articulate economic alternatives.

Robbie Gillett is an organiser with the Reclaim the Power network and campaigner at CTC – the national cycling charity. He was previously involved with the Barton Moss Anti-Fracking Camp, Plane Stupid, the Camp for Climate Action and the University of Manchester Students' Union.

References

1. George Osborne's speech to Conservative Party conference, October 2011.
2. The 'Big Six' are most commonly cited as British Gas, EDF Energy, npower, E.ON UK, Scottish Power and SSE.
3. Talk Fracking – http://www.talkfracking.org/resources/
4. Lock the Gate Alliance – http://www.lockthegate.org.au/
5. Balcombe Parish Council, Fracking Poll Results, September 2012. https://balcombeparishcouncil.files.wordpress.com/2012/10/fracking-poll-results.pdf
6. 'Policing Balcombe: was operation designed to deter protesters?', Netpol, May 2014. https://netpol.org/2014/05/13/policing-balcombe-part-1/
7. Unite the Union policy against fracking, 2014. http://www.unitetheunion.org/uploaded/documents/Decisions%20of%20the%20Policy%20Conference%20201411-21375.pdf
8. Reclaim the Power – www.nodashforgas.org.uk
9. 'Did the protests at Balcombe have an impact on public perceptions of shale gas?' Nottingham University. http://nottspolitics.org/2013/10/01/did-the-protests-at-balcombe-have-an-impact-on-public-perceptions-of-shale-gas/
10. Adam Ramsay, 'Green membership overtakes Lib Dems and UKIP. Here's 13 reasons why', Open Democracy, January 2015. https://www.opendemocracy.net/ourkingdom/adam-ramsay/green-membership-overtakes-lib-dems-and-ukip-here%27s-13-reasons-why
11. Global Divestment – http://gofossilfree.org/commitments/

Securing nature's future: why conservation needs a youth movement

Matt Adam Williams

It's mid-December, four o'clock in the afternoon, and the temperature has just dropped below zero. The clouds are stained pink. The sky is barely visible, obscured by millions of tiny black bodies, painting their own pointillist piece against the sunset. The swirling flocks of star-lings are gathering over Somerset's reedbeds to roost for the night, as they do every evening in the winter.

Just when I don't think this moment could be any more magical, two otter cubs appear in the water in front of us and begin playing, tussling for first place as they race each other to the water's edge. The little light there is left at this late winter hour is reflected in the sheen of their wet, matted coats of fur. I can't feel my hands any more; the still air bites at my fingertips.

This is the most cherished wildlife moment of my life so far. It's one among many memories; I'm extremely privileged to have spent my life watching and following animals. This passion has taken me to moun-tains on Scottish islands and to the depths of jungles on the island of Borneo.

Our British Isles boast a proud tradition of exploring and docu-menting nature, and they're home to some of the world's most wonderful wildlife spectacles.

But the arrayed horsemen of the ecological apocalypse, including intensive farming, overuse of resources, climate change and loss of habitat, are charging down on the natural world. These four factors place extra pressures on wildlife and at the same time make the space for it smaller and less hospitable. Very often, the root cause of these pressures can be traced back to the scale and nature of our consump-tion of resources from nature – whether it's for food, for consumer goods or for energy.

This is particularly bad news for young people, who will be growing old with the consequences. When we reach retirement age, will any turtle doves still purr in the UK countryside, or will we only remember them on the second day of Christmas? Will kestrels still hover over field margins hunting for voles, their brown and black tortoiseshell plumage glistening in the sun?

In 1980, the Brundtland Commission published a landmark report defining 'sustainable development', as development which 'meets the needs of the present without compromising the ability of future generations to meet their own needs'.[1] The natural environment and the climate are, in a sense, held 'in trust' by those in power, for young people and for future generations. But those in power are betraying that trust by wrecking the climate and ransacking nature. Young people are being handed a raw deal.

What's more, today's young people are less connected to nature than any previous generation. To paraphrase David Attenborough, people don't care about what they don't experience, and they don't protect what they don't care about. This is bad news for nature, as well as people, and could in fact be the biggest long-term threat to conservation. If young people today aren't invested in nature, even fewer people will care enough to stand up for it in the future.

This isn't to deny that the past few decades have seen a growing legal recognition of the importance of the natural environment. Sites which are important for wildlife can, thanks to various bits of European and UK legislation, be designated as Sites of Special Scientific Interest (SSSI), Special Areas of Conservation and Special Protection Areas. This should put them beyond the reach of development, and prioritises them for conservation action from public bodies and charities.

Wildlife NGOs have also seen their support blossom, with the National Trust and Royal Society for the Protection for Birds (RSPB) now boasting millions of members. The RSPB has around 200,000 members under the age of eighteen. And large audiences tune into programmes like *Springwatch* and David Attenborough's documentaries.

Targeted interventions have brought bird species like bitterns and red kites back from the brink of extinction in the UK. Now, a red kite circling over the UK countryside is almost as commonplace as it was a couple of centuries ago. A bittern skulking among the long stems of a reedbed might be very hard to see, but it's no longer a rarity in the UK.

Regardless of all this progress, the natural world is doing worse than ever. Young people will inherit a very different countryside from the one that their grandparents grew up in. The 2010 international target for halting the decline in biodiversity was missed and pushed back to 2020 (Aichi Biodiversity Targets). That target also looks set to be missed by a long way.

Even though the UK Government is signed up to powerful European and national legislation to protect wildlife, developers frequently put it to the test. Boris Johnson's suggested airport in the Thames Estuary would have meant building over areas protected under European law for their wildlife value. The proposed building was thrown out by the Government's independent Airports Commission. Celtique Energy recently applied to frack for gas in the South Downs National Park – but were rejected by the local planning authority. But attacks like these are mounting.

Developers are also testing the designations of these pieces of land. A local authority wants to build 5000 homes on an SSSI that is home to 1 per cent of the UK's breeding population of nightingales. If approved, this would be the largest loss of SSSI land in several decades. Regardless of the eventual decision on this, it shows that designated statuses like SSSI don't stop developers from chancing their luck.

The landmark *State of Nature* report in 2013, a collaboration by the conservation sector, showed that of the species surveyed, 60 per cent had declined in the last 50 years, around one third of them severely.

New research has also showed that it is our more common species that are really suffering. Birds like starlings and sparrows that live on vast countryside areas (mostly farmland), beyond direct management by conservation NGOs, are plummeting in numbers. There are now 421 million fewer birds in European skies than there were in the 1980s. Systemic changes to the countryside that affect ubiquitous species are harder to tackle because they require system change, not niche interventions.

Worryingly, conservationists are adopting some of the thinking of the very system that is causing this ecological destruction.

Wildlife NGOs are exploring how incorporating nature into the market can provide ways to appease business and developers. Ecosystem services are processes such as water filtering and carbon storage, which nature provides free of charge. But many think that properly recognising the value of these services in the economy would help to make the case for protecting nature.

Biodiversity offsetting describes the creation of new green space in one location theoretically to compensate for the destruction other green space that needs to be developed. So, for example, plant hundreds of new trees and you might be allowed to get away with destroying an ancient woodland.

Both of these concepts are (not without some controversy) increasingly gaining traction within the formal conservation sector. In some cases, this can mean that special places are more likely to be protected. In other cases, these ideas might allow private interests to fiddle the numbers in favour of developing special places. Some environmentalists think these approaches are key, while others think they are risky. For example, a long-running debate between Tony Juniper and George Monbiot, both renowned environmental campaigners, illustrates the level of division.

Wider society has also shifted towards supporting the values of a free-market, neoliberal economy in recent decades. Community ties have become weaker; individuals are increasingly described as consumers, not citizens; nature and its processes are often viewed as a commodity. Our lives are increasingly bracketed by the money we earn, the hours we work and the goods we buy.

Our lives, particularly those of children, are also increasingly domesticated. Young people in particular spend less and less time outdoors and more time in their bedrooms in front of screens. In 2009, only 10 per cent of children played in a natural area, compared to 40 per cent in the 1970s.

Stephen Moss, lifelong naturalist and author of the *Natural Childhood* report, believes that we are in danger of raising successive generations of children and young people who are largely disconnected not just from nature, but from the simple joys of outdoor play:

> Our children should be free-range, allowed to explore the wider world on their own or with friends from an early age. Instead we wrap them in metaphorical layers of cotton wool, confine them to home and keep them constantly in sight to justify our (mostly unwarranted) fears for them. Yet by depriving them of contact with the natural world, we are endangering both their futures and that of the world itself.[2]

On top of this, our neighbourhoods have changed, becoming more transient and atomised. As people's working lives become less stable we are less likely to live in any one place for an extended period of time. We are less connected to the people we live with and the places we live in.[3] Children's contact with nature has been steadily declining for a number of decades. Since the 1970s the area around a child's home where they are allowed to play, walk and explore has declined by 90 per cent and children are now usually only allowed out if accompanied by an adult.[4] Parents feel more afraid to allow their children into our public space, which has been allowed to deteriorate. Rubbish, abandoned cars, fear of strangers and traffic all deter parents from letting their children roam. Children themselves report being scared to go outside. The rhetoric of fear and security and especially of 'stranger danger' in much of our media has understandably exacerbated many parents' reluctance to let their children roam free outdoors.

Many experts have examined the links between changes in government policy and the decline in urban green spaces. Writer and horticulturalist Dr Noel Kingsbury told me that in many places 'green space had become a blight'.[5] According to Kingsbury, the cause of this is central government attacks on local government, which reduced funding for public parks. Under Margaret Thatcher, compulsory competitive tendering meant that the management of parks had to be sold off to the highest bidding private companies. This resulted in a sharp drop off in expertise and knowledge about how to manage parks and their plants, then in the quality of public green space and also in the opportunities for young people to be apprentices and work their way up the park management system.

Decline in the availability and quality of green spaces affects children's emotional, mental and physical health. Crucially, they also reduce children's contact with and their interest in nature. This makes it even less likely that they will care about and want to protect nature when they are older, and harms nature's prospects in the long-term.

This doesn't mean that young people don't care, quite the opposite. Research conducted by the youth volunteering charity V showed that in a group of 1000 sixteen to twenty-five year olds, over 50 per cent were 'very concerned' about terrorism, war, poverty, famine and climate change. In their local areas, 35 per cent were 'very concerned' by the quality of the environment and 42 per cent by a lack of activities to get involved in. However, exactly 50 per cent also responded that they were unsure how to help.[6]

Children's 'attachment to place, civic engagement and environmental stewardship' are all enhanced by environmental education.[7] Knowledge and understanding are also reported to increase thanks to access to the outdoors. Young people's health can benefit from more access to the outdoors, reducing levels or stress and improving mental wellbeing. There is evidence that ADHD symptoms can be reduced by 30 per cent in children who have access to nature.[8] Time spent outdoors is also the strongest link with levels of physical activity, and childhood attitudes to exercise are strongly predictive of levels of physical activity in adulthood.[9]

So, at the same time as wildlife is more at risk than ever, young people's connection to it is also at a very low ebb. This is perhaps the biggest threat to the long-term health of conservation. When today's young people are adults, the value they place on nature will determine whether and how they choose to protect it.

Conservation organisations aren't twiddling their thumbs. The National Trust and RSPB, among others, have undertaken a number of huge initiatives to tackle the problem of young people's relationship with nature, including the Natural Childhood report, *50 Things to Do before you're 11¾* and the subsequent founding of the Wild Network, a collection of over 1700 organisations working to connect young people and families with the outdoors.

But perhaps the most exciting prospect for change comes from young people. For several years now, a growing international youth climate change movement has sprung up in countries across the world, from the US to India, Canada, the UK, Australia, Taiwan, Kenya and many, many others. Young people have taken ownership of the fact that climate change will affect their lives for decades to come, due to the decisions of political leaders and fossil fuel companies today. Organisations like 350.org and the UK Youth Climate Coalition, and campaigns like the one for fossil fuel divestment, have revolutionised the international climate change scene. The youth climate change movement has become a powerful political force, gaining respect and legitimacy, precisely because young people are the ones who will inherit the world created by today's decisions.

There is also an emerging young drive toward natural conservation. Organisations like A Focus on Nature and Next Generation Birders, led by and for young people, are at the heart of a new young network of naturalists. Lucy McRobert, 24, Creative Director of A Focus on Nature, the UK's leading youth conservation organisation, says: 'Young people are the biggest hope for the natural world right now. The passion and enthusiasm of a new wave of conservationists and naturalists reassure me that nature has a fighting chance'.[10] This community of committed young naturalists and wildlife photographers isn't yet a movement for change. But it could be.

The next step is for these organisations to find their political voice, and to tell politicians and business leaders that they want to inherit a flourishing natural world. And if current leaders aren't going to guarantee that for them then they need to step aside and let young people – with their magnifying glasses, notebooks and chainsaws in hand – do it for themselves.

Matt Williams is a lifelong wildlife lover, a conservationist and a photographer. A former Co-Director of the UK Youth Climate Coalition, he now helps run A Focus on Nature, the UK's leading youth conservation network, organised by and for young people. Follow him @mattadamw and mattadamwilliams.co.uk.

Notes

1. *Report of the World Commission on Environment and Development: Our Common Future*, 1980.
2. Stephen Moss, personal communication, 2015.
3. Ruth Davis, 'A Popular Environmentalism', *Soundings* 51 (2012).
4. Stephen Moss, *Natural Childhood*, National Trust, 2012.
5. Dr Noel Kingsbury, personal communication, 2014.
6. Vinformed, *Barriers preventing passionate young people acting on their concerns*, 2007.
7. RSPB, *Every Child Outdoors: Summary Report*, 2007.
8. *Ibid.*
9. *Ibid.*
10. Lucy McRobert, personal communication, 2014.

Going mainstream: counter culture and alternative media

Deborah Grayson

Whether we're being defined by what we are – the 'Facebook genera-tion', the 'selfie generation', 'digital natives' – or what we are not (newspaper readers, TV watchers) young peoples' media use is seen as having profound political consequences. Discussions of our genera-tion invariably mention our media habits, and these accounts tend to veer between wild optimism and deep pessimism. Either new tech-nologies have the potential to open up space for radical alternatives, or corporations have won, with individualised young people only inter-ested in the 'Daily Me'.

This reflects a general yo-yoing back and forth within media theory between utopian and dystopian visions of the effects of digital media – either they'll bring in an era of world peace, global understanding and democratic empowerment, or we'll become even more enslaved to capitalism, under constant surveillance from both corporations and states. Recent books such as *Misunderstanding the Internet* have made the more nuanced (and perhaps obvious) point that context matters: other factors will contribute to whether new media technologies are liberatory or oppressive.[1]

This chapter is the attempt to provide some of that context for young people and radical politics in the UK today. First, it makes the case that 'going mainstream' is both possible and desirable. Then it looks at the current state of play, as media power has both become more fragmented and more concentrated over recent years. It addresses the major reason for the continued dominance of big corpo-rate media providers – the 'myth of the mediated centre'. What alternative media could or should look like in that context is explored by looking at two alternative news sources: Indymedia and openDe-mocracy. The need for institutions and some hierarchy of knowledge and political education is then discussed in relation to the Palestine solidarity movement.

From margins to mainstream

Most of Britain's private media are owned by large corporations, which are deeply invested in neoliberalism and will resist any significant challenge to it.[2] The BBC, which is still the dominant news provider, is too timid and too in thrall to our corrupted politics to allow much space for wholesale critiques of the system. Whatever resistance we build will have to originate from the margins.

Yet at the same time, if we want to see serious change, whatever we build from the margins can't *remain* marginal. In a sense, this process is already underway. Global events have upped the profile of protest, with waves of unrest around the world since the 2008 financial crisis. This has contributed to a renewed sense that resistance might have a relationship with popular culture, as when a masked and anonymous protester was named Time Magazine's Person of the Year 2011. Even in the more muted context of the UK, active dissent has become considerably more normalised in the last five years, particularly since the student protests of 2010-11, and, rather differently, the 2011 riots.

That said, we in the UK have so far seen nothing like the mass gatherings seen in Tahrir Square, Gezi Park or Hong Kong, or the creative re-imaginings of what economic and social life could look like – as seen in Spain and Greece – apart from in Scotland where the organising around the independence referendum instigated a vibrant, widespread conversation about what kind of country Scotland wants to be. Elsewhere in the UK, and in England particularly, that envisioning remains in isolated pockets: while participating in protest is no longer the preserve of 'crazies', working collectively towards a mutually imagined world is far from mainstream.

If we want it to become so, this raises the question of what kinds of communications we should be producing ourselves, and what relationships are desirable with the media institutions that dominate our lives.

There has always been a strand of radical politics which rejects corporate media altogether as a set of institutions which will inevitably corrupt and taint the intended message. While this is arguably true, it also places real limitations on the scale of the political project. As a member of the new Spanish party Podemos put it:

Television is where the bulk of public opinion in any country is built. If you decide that you don't want to access that space on principal, what you're saying is that you give up the democratic path to win elections.[3]

If we believe in democracy, we have to find some way of interacting with institutions like television, given their influence on public life, even as we critique them and seek to establish alternatives.

The lay of the land

Changes in media use have broadly reflected other changes in society in the post-war era, as backgrounds, lifestyles and working lives have become more diverse. Over that period, political party membership has declined from about 6 per cent of the population in 1953 to 0.8 per cent today, and trade union membership has halved from its peak of over 13 million in 1979 to 6.5 million in 2013.

At the same time, digitisation has seen a transformation in media consumption habits, with a fragmentation of the huge audiences of the early days of mass communications media. In the 1950s, 88 per cent of people in Britain read a daily newspaper; today this is around 40 per cent. And televised events such as the Royal Wedding in 2011 or the Olympics opening ceremony in 2012 can still attract 25 million+ viewers, but this was the kind of audience size that popular entertainment shows could draw back in the days of two or three television channels. Today, shows like *Doctor Who* are doing well if they get audiences of 8 million.

Since the 1950s, then, mass audiences have gradually fragmented across a wide variety of mediums and platforms: satellite and digital TV channels, pirate, community and digital radio stations, and the internet, hosting text, video and audio content. This, combined with the falling costs of digital production and the ease of sharing provided by social media platforms, has helped countercultural and radical movements to share information and coordinate action (although the potential power of 'new technology' is nothing new – the photocopier played a similar role in information sharing in the 1980s).

Despite this huge increase in communications media and channels, mainstream media have maintained, and in some ways strengthened, their dominance. TV was still the primary source of news for three quarters of British people in 2013, the majority of that from a single channel, BBC1. Age does make a difference: young people are less likely to rely on TV or newspapers than older people, and more likely to use the internet or apps.[4] But online news, too, is overwhelmingly concentrated amongst 'legacy' news organisations, particularly the BBC, *The Guardian* and the *Daily Mail*, as well as content aggregators like Yahoo and Google. While increasing numbers of young people say they get their news from social media platforms, research with students has found that the links being shared are also predominantly established sources, and that it is generally the same stories and content that are being seen whether they're being accessed via Facebook, Snapchat or Vine.[5]

What we're seeing are two simultaneous and contradictory trends: towards both fragmentation and concentration. While there is no shortage of alternative *content*, most of it speaks to very small audiences, and where more substantial audiences do exist they are often poorly networked. Even the proliferation of social media platforms may be increasing the advantage of established sources who can spare the resources to work out how to interact with them. Small campaigns and NGOs will typically have a Facebook and Twitter presence, but they don't always also have a strategy for YouTube, Instagram and Tumblr, or find time to identify relevant vloggers who could help promote their work. The recent launch of Snapchat Discover, a news service directly accessible within the app, is a case in point: rather than giving users the opportunity to choose their own sources, they are automatically pointed to a small number of preselected partners, including CNN, Yahoo News and the *Daily Mail*.

Perhaps there is a parallel to be drawn with the political parties. Labour and the Conservatives are suffering from a long-term decline in support, each polling between 30-35 per cent of the vote for the last few years. Neither is anywhere near having the support of the majority of the electorate, and given low voter turnout they were already getting well below 50 per cent of the vote *between them* in 2010.[6] Nonetheless, they remain the most well-organised and coherent political forces that we have – with the collapse of the Liberal Democrat vote there is no one else who comes close to being able to mobilise and coordinate more than 8 million people to vote in a unified way and therefore gain democratic legitimacy. Similarly, declines in audience share don't necessarily result in a loss of significance of mainstream and legacy media if they consistently draw together more people than any other single sources. There may be more and more people who are looking askance at what they see on TV or simply ignoring what's being said in the papers, but these two media remain the most mainstream sources we have.

The myth of the mediated centre

This continued dominance is no accident. Media have a particular kind of power because they not only get to tell the stories of others, but can frame and shape their own stories, particularly to trumpet their own importance. This is what media academic Nick Couldry calls 'the myth of the mediated centre'.[7] Much early work within media studies saw society in similar terms to Émile Durkheim – as made up of different parts that became integrated into a functional whole. Durkheim thought that this integration took place, in traditional societies, through religious rituals. In modern societies, so this line of thinking went, it was mass media institutions that gave us a sense of common identity and common purpose. But Couldry argues otherwise: it isn't that mass media institutions *actually* integrate society, it's that *they relentlessly tell us that they do*.

This is a crucial part of the power that our legacy media institutions wield over us. Every day they are able to pump out the message, both implicitly and explicitly, that *what they are talking about is what is important*, be that benefit scroungers, lazy immigrants, Kim Kardashian's derrière or Ed Miliband's face when he's eating a sandwich. The flip-side of this is that what you *don't* see in the media – deaths in detention centres, secret trade deals between the EU and US, or the tax affairs of newspaper owners – are automatically *unimportant*. By portraying themselves as the beating heart of British life they gain a huge amount of power, not only to set the news agenda but also to define who is an A or Z list celebrity, which comedians have enough of a profile to be invited onto TV panel shows (clue: mostly white men), and which people, ideas and ways of life need to be taken into account by 'everybody'. This simultaneously defines what can be ignored.

In liberal media theory, the circular tendency of media institutions to say 'whatever we're talking about is all there is to talk about' is supposed to be counterbalanced by the search for novelty, the desire to get the scoop or be the first to discover the next big thing. But mainstream media are remarkably homogenous in the topics they cover and the framing they use, with TV news editors starting the day by looking at what's in the newspapers, and those newspapers, particular online editions, poaching each other's stories and reproducing corporate press releases in the set of practices known as 'churnalism'. This groupthink across much of the industry is most visible when it comes to questions of their own behaviour, such as the hacking scandal, where for years the allegations remained confined to *The Guardian*. Despite being in intense competition with one another, none of the other tabloids chose to run with this story until the revelations about Milly Dowler's voicemail being hacked made it unignorable.

This is the mountain that alternative media have to climb. Practically speaking, it is difficult to build an audience of any significant size in a noisy environment in which wealthy media institutions have a considerable advantage. And whatever story you're trying to tell has to also account for why, if it is so relevant to a popular audience, the mainstream media aren't talking about it already. Even an internet star like Zoella, whose 7 million YouTube subscribers constitute a larger audience than much of primetime TV, still had to pass through the heavily controlled and commercialised symbolic centre of mass media institutions in order to link that audience with a wider public. There are, as yet, few bridging points for diverse and minority media to connect with one another. Consequently it is very hard to challenge the perception that if you aren't 'in the media' you can't have anything of importance to say.

This is not to say that there are no possibilities for influencing or even altering the mainstream narrative. But it is only by having a realistic understanding of the difficulties and limitations of starting from the margins that we can understand how to exploit those openings when they arise. The next section looks at this in relation to two alternative news providers, Indymedia and openDemocracy.

Another news as possible

Indymedia UK was founded by a group of people brought together by the Reclaim the Streets protest parties and the alter-globalisation movement. It emerged out of the global network of independent media collectives established after the Seattle protests against the

World Trade Organisation in 1999. The format is based on the principle of open publishing. In the words of their mission statement, Indymedia aims to erode 'the dividing line between reporters and reported, between active producers and passive audiences: people are able to speak for themselves'.[8] In line with their anti-capitalist stance, they set themselves up in opposition to corporate news providers in a number of ways: taking no payments, running no adverts, allowing anonymous posting, and also having no editors in the traditional sense. Although the regional sites around the world and around the UK vary in their policies – some allow unmoderated posts, while others check that content meets a set of guidelines before uploading to the main newswire – as much leeway as possible is given to those who want to post.

The thinking behind this kind of media emerged out of the experience of seeing protests profoundly misrepresented by mainstream news providers. Rather than lobbying those organisations to write more accurate journalism, the idea was that activists should tell the truth by uploading their own stories and videos to a non-corporate space. In their early days the sites were highly innovative, with interactive features like self-publishing, and organising through wikis, which later spread across the web. However, as the internet developed and, especially as corporate social media took off, the platform has struggled to maintain its audience. In 2012, the London collective announced it was discontinuing its activities, although elsewhere in the UK, groups do continue to host and moderate content.

The London collective's reasons provide a useful insight into the difficulties of creating alternative platforms.[9] One big factor was the growth of Twitter, Facebook and YouTube as the default places to host and post content. Despite being well aware that these sites mine our data and regularly close down 'suspicious' accounts, it has proved hard to persuade even committed anti-capitalists and anarchists to forego them altogether. Partly, corporate networking sites are extremely easy to use and have a lot of useful and appealing functions; perhaps too there has been a growing recognition that they are better tools for building an audience beyond a core of activists who can easily end up just talking to themselves. The London collective also cited activist burnout, an inability to respond to events quickly enough, and problems with other Indymedia sites. In some areas a lack of moderation had allowed pieces attacking particular groups and individuals to be posted to the main newswire, and because the different collectives acted autonomously it was often impossible to get them removed.[10]

The online magazine openDemocracy was founded in 2000, at around the same time as Indymedia, and makes for an interesting contrast. Although not a large organisation, it does have enough of a resource base to pay staff to write and edit content. While still a minority news source, it has considerably higher traffic rankings than Indymedia – the latter is roughly ranked about 66,000 in the most visited sites in the UK, openDemocracy is number 5020. (To put both of those into perspective, the *Daily Mail* ranks fourteenth and *The Guardian* sixteenth.)[11]

Unlike Indymedia, openDemocracy has not set itself up in *opposition* to mainstream news sources, although it does often run content which is highly critical of them. It is reasonably well networked with mainstream institutions and journalists, and occasionally breaks stories which then make their way into the wider news agenda. Those who come from the kind of tradition that produced Indymedia might argue that the stories which do cross over will only ever be those which conform to mainstream news values, and which leave the 'mediated centre' unchallenged. Something of this dynamic could be seen around political commentator Peter Oborne's resignation from the *Telegraph* over allegations that the newspaper had suppressed details of HSBC's tax avoidance schemes. Although the story broke in openDemocracy,[12] HSBC's tax affairs were already in the news, and Oborne himself is a well-known journalist with a national profile. This is indeed the usual relationship between minority and mainstream news providers – those on the margins can add more detail to an existing narrative, but find it very hard to set the agenda themselves.

Yet there was a more interesting, unusual example at the beginning of 2015, when openDemocracy managed to play a more active role in opening up space for radical politics by covering the 'green surge'. At the time, the Green party was regularly in the news in relation to who should take part in the general election TV debates, but in keeping with the general bias towards two-party politics, the mainstream story was mostly focused on the implications for David Cameron or Ed Miliband if the Greens did or did not take part. The openDemocracy piece,[13] written by *Resist!* contributor and Green party member Adam Ramsay, revealed that the UK Green Parties were about to overtake UKIP and the Lib Dems in terms of party membership. This *changed* the story, fuelling first an even bigger rise in membership, and then helping to shift the focus to the Greens' manifesto pledges. The following week saw substantial pieces on their policies in the *Telegraph* and *The Times*, as well as an appearance by Green leader Natalie Bennett on the BBC's Sunday Politics show – all of which, for better or worse, focused largely on the Greens' economic policies.

What can we learn from these two examples of alternative media? First, neither has come anywhere near to becoming a major news provider. Although both have played an important role in helping to coordinate action among like-minded people, they still have to rely on mainstream organisations if they want to communicate a message to a broader audience. Perhaps this will change over the next decade or two, but this is the current reality. This doesn't mean that alternative media providers are unnecessary – as we've seen, it is possible, although rare, for them to open up space in a mainstream context for radical ideas. In addition, they play an important role in building resilience in the wider movement. From Indymedia, we have an important reminder that what a lot of people think of as their own 'personal' social media space is itself corporate space, and we should use it with caution. We are in a dangerous position if most of the political activity in the country could be stopped on a whim by Facebook and Google.

The second thing to learn is that having an income stream matters. At the root of the difficulties faced by the London Indymedia collective lay a basic constraint around time and resources. The site always depended on volunteers to moderate and approve content, fix bugs and write new code, and source spaces, computers and equipment – and volunteers have other commitments and can't always be on the spot to respond to stories as they happen, or to remove offensive and divisive posts. openDemocracy has a more stable resource base, although constant rounds of fundraising are required to keep it afloat. The sustainability of alternative news media over the coming years will to a large extent depend on finding new ways to support them financially.

Finally, there is the question of the role of editors and moderators in the potentially limitless space of the internet. The ideal behind open publishing and enabling people to 'speak for themselves' is instinctively admirable, but the problems faced by Indymedia show its limitations. People speaking for themselves is only a meaningful concept if there is an audience to hear them – and equally, it is always possible that the thing they want to say is harmful, dangerous or simply irrelevant. A lack of moderation on some Indymedia sites damaged the whole project, undermining trust, which is the basis for collective action. In the next section, we will look at the case of the Palestine solidarity movement, where this kind of 'editing' has been essential to the success of the counter-narrative.

Building a counter-narrative: Palestine solidarity

The response to the attacks in Gaza in the summer of 2014 was described as a breakthrough by many long-standing Palestine solidarity activists. Among the horror of 2000 people being killed, a third of them children, there was a sense of the tide turning against Israel's aggression, certainly in a more significant way than during the attacks of 2009 and 2012.

Social media and digital technology were generally credited with a major role in this. They allowed people on the ground to record and report their experiences directly; they gave mainstream journalists the means of reporting on the spot rather than having to run everything through their editors; and they gave a wider audience the opportunity to critique what they saw as biased reporting. The unprecedented number of people out on the streets at the various Palestine demonstrations showed that solidarity activists had managed not only to convince significant numbers that the mainstream media narrative was *wrong*, but that their alternative was *right* – and was credible enough to motivate people into action.

Dynamics around trust in the media are strange. We know in general terms that journalists are less trusted than estate agents, and although not all mediums have the rock-bottom ratings of the tabloids, trust in broadsheet journalists declined from 65 per cent in 2003 to 38 per cent in 2013.[14] The BBC, while slightly more trusted, saw a decline over the same period from 81 per cent to 44 per cent, mostly as a result of the Iraq war.[15] At the same time, dominant media framings, particularly around immigration and welfare, are reproduced on radio phone-in shows and in discussion forums on a daily basis – and even the largest demonstrations against austerity or the financial sector have been nowhere near the size of the mobilisations in Greece or Spain. Even moving people from a passive mistrust in the media to thinking 'maybe they're wrong to think that immigrants are to blame' is a challenge, let alone mobilising active resistance.

Taking action requires *conviction,* particularly if you're likely to face oppressive reactions like police violence in response. Conviction, rather than doubt, is hard to build from the margins. If the status quo is in your favour, it can be a very successful tactic to use 'uncertainty' to prevent or delay action, from the tobacco companies sowing the seeds of doubt about the link between cigarette smoking and lung cancer, to the oil industry undermining the consensus around the role of human carbon emissions in destabilising the climate. The Israeli propaganda machine has benefited from this as well. Whether or not their hardline narratives are really believed is not necessarily the point, so long as most of the audience comes away thinking the situation is so complex that it is best left alone. A classic example of this was the widely-shared Huffington Post article '7 Things to Consider Before Choosing Sides in the Middle East Conflict' which did the rounds during the incursion, ending by suggesting people take the side of 'humous'.[16] But it was this liberal consensus that began to crack in the summer of 2014.

What makes this a particularly interesting case is that the Palestine solidarity movement has not only had to counter messages being relayed by mainstream media, but also those emanating from conspiracy theorists. Conspiracies have an obvious appeal for those who have started questioning mainstream narratives and who have begun to get an inkling of the extent of the lies and corruption that the powerful use to maintain their power. Yet they pose obvious dangers for movements, either because they lead people towards the extreme reactions – the EDL, for example, was fuelled by conspiracy theories about the way that 'Muslim atrocities' were being covered up – or, more likely, because they undermine the basis of any kind of collective action.

Of course, just because you're paranoid doesn't mean they're not out to get you, and some of the cases labelled as 'conspiracies' probably are genuine cover-ups, such as the apparent suicide of the Iraq war whistle-blower David Kelly. But the classic form of a conspiracy theory is similar to the 'uncertainty principle' used by the tobacco industry – deconstructing a partial selection of the facts, inviting the audience to 'question everything', and ending with something along the lines of 'maybe this isn't true, but how can you be sure?' This is a poor basis for motivating people to support targeted actions, such as the Boycott, Divestment and Sanctions movement, which might actually be effective at pressuring the Israeli state to reduce its violence.

Part of what has worked to counter this within the solidarity movement has been a strong commitment to some basic journalistic values, particularly cross-checking facts and corroborating with sources on the ground. Institutions like online magazine Electronic Intifada acted as gatekeepers during Operation Protective Edge, counteracting misinformation not only from pro-Israeli sources but also within the movement, including ensuring that pictures being circulated were actually from Gaza rather than Syria or elsewhere. In addition, information was fed through trusted networks such as faith groups or relationships built by the anti-war movement. Well-established solidarity activists provided support for groups newly politicised by the incursion, in which they shared key points, like ensuring that criticism of Israel didn't slip into anti-Semitism.

This example is important because the Palestine solidarity movement is the entry point into politics for many people, particularly young people. It shows that creating a strong counter-narrative does in fact require a certain amount of hierarchy, where those with more knowledge and experience are able to pass that on to newcomers. Of course, this shouldn't be done in an authoritarian way, but without targeted information sharing it isn't possible to tell a collective story. When you know a single anti-Semitic poster can discredit a demonstration of thousands, a certain amount of care over communication becomes essential. This kind of political education can be done effectively through minority news sources and the judicious use of corporate social media — but only if there are institutions able to validate and accredit certain voices over others, rather than a free-for-all.

Conclusions

To conclude, I want to draw a few lessons from the examples discussed. The first is that institutions matter. Personal social media do sometimes break into the mainstream, but always as *reactions* to what is already being talked about. They invariably do not set the agenda or break a story. Our Twitter accounts and Wordpress blogs are themselves part of a corporate media environment, with all of the limitations that entails. As difficult as it is to reshape the mainstream story, it is occasionally possible for a small-scale organisation to do — whereas as an individual it is almost impossible, unless you've already passed through 'the centre' as a journalist or celebrity.

A second related point is that if institutions matter, money also matters. Journalism as a paid profession remains crucially important. In a sense 'anyone' can tell their own story, but for it to be heard it needs to be well researched and credible, and there needs to be an audience. The sustainability of alternative news providers will depend on whether we can find new forms of revenue generation for content – a tricky one, given the pervasive culture of 'free' access online (which effectively means the audience being sold to advertisers). However, there may be a way of shifting that culture by linking small payments to online privacy, where data will not be stored. Without some means of financially supporting alternative media we will struggle to build and maintain institutions of any longevity.

This chapter has largely focused on news media – another whole article would be required to properly address entertainment media and popular culture, although these are crucial areas for building counter-narratives. This is where we can see the problem posed by the fragmentation of minority audiences very clearly. Alternative comedy, for example, has become increasingly political, with comedians such as Josie Long attracting substantial audiences. On the other hand, someone like MC Akala can draw 2 million views on YouTube for a rant about race, police violence, the privatisation of prisons and our colonial past.[17] The meeting point for the former's mostly white middle-class audience and Akala's working-class, racially diverse fans would be a powerful thing, but at the moment they are only likely to have any point of crossover in the corporate mainstream. Connecting up those audiences without having to pass through 'the centre' is a potential avenue for a radical future.

Finally, although it won't be easy, there is still everything to play for. Being realistic about what is currently possible is a better starting point for building genuine alternatives than dreaming of 'free media' and being endlessly disappointed when it fails. With a clear understanding of the current state of the media we can identify the cracks in the system. By taking the opportunities they offer, we can build effective counter-narratives to neoliberalism.

Deborah Grayson is an academic and activist. After a few years of campaigning groups like Climate Rush, Yes to Fairer Votes and the Media Reform Coalition, she is now taking some time to think by doing a Ph.D. in the Department of Media and Communications at Goldsmiths. Her research examines the role of media technologies in how people form beliefs and knowledge about the world, which she is looking at through a collaboration with a charity. If you're interested in non-mainstream sources of news and comment, she would recommend sites like:

Novara Media – video, audio and text content addressing a variety of social and economic issues http://novaramedia.com/

Another Angry Voice – blog and shareable memes, mostly covering the case against austerity http://anotherangryvoice.blogspot.co.uk/

Bite News – YouTube channel for youth democracy movement Bite the Ballot https://www.youtube.com/channel/UCN0pTmLZ8YHygLxGLcBLa9g

Bella Caledonia – newspaper and website that was central to the independence campaign in Scotland, and continues to cover radical politics north of the border http://bellacaledonia.org.uk/

Resonance FM – arts radio project with a radical twist based in London http://resonancefm.com/

The Conversation – an independent source of news and views from academics and researchers http://theconversation.com/uk

Weekly Economics Podcast – podcast looking at current issues in economics in normal-person language https://soundcloud.com/weeklyeconomicspodcast

Notes

1. James Curran, Natalie Fenton and Des Freedman, *Misunderstanding the Internet*, London, 2011.
2. This is not only in terms of their media operations, but also in terms of other corporate interests such as Rupert Murdoch's education investments in the US.
3. Bécquer Seguín and Sebastiaan Faber, 'Can Podemos win in Spain?', *The Nation*, 2 February 2015. http://www.thenation.com/article/195129/can-podemos-win-spain
4. Ofcom 2013: 90 per cent of over fifty-fives rely on TV, 54 per cent on newspapers, 21 per cent use the internet/apps. For sixteen to twenty-four year-olds, 59 per cent rely on TV, 33 per cent on newspapers, 60 per cent use the internet/apps. http://stakeholders.ofcom.org.uk/binaries/research/tv-research/news/News_Report_2013.pdf
5. Angela Phillips, 'Accessing and Consuming News: How Young People Find News in a Networked Society', Communities and Culture Network, June 2014. http://www.communitiesandculture.org/files/2014/10/Accessing-News-Final-Report2.pdf

6. In the 2010 election, the Conservatives got 10.7 million votes and Labour 8.6 million votes, out of 45.6 million registered voters. Given that an estimated 5 million eligible voters are missing from the register, fewer than 40 per cent of British citizens actually endorsed *either* Labour *or* the Tories.

7. For more on this see Couldry's book *Media Rituals*, London, 2012.

8. 'IMC UK Mission Statement', Indymedia UK, 25 June 2003. http://www.indymedia.org.uk/en/static/mission.html

9. 'Time to move on: IMC London signing off' Indymedia UK, 13 October 2012. http://www.indymedia.org.uk/en/2012/10/501214.html

10. 'Why Indymedia sucks – Thoughts from conference 09', Indymedia London, 7 June 2009. http://london.indymedia.org/articles/1541

11. Figures retrieved from http://www.alexa.com/ February 2015.

12. Peter Oborne, 'Why I have resigned from *The Telegraph*', OpenDemocracy, 17 February 2015. https://www.opendemocracy.net/ourkingdom/peter-oborne/why-i-have-resigned-from-telegraph

13. Adam Ramsay, 'Another note on party memberships in the UK', OpenDemocracy, 14 January 2015. https://www.opendemocracy.net/ourkingdom/adam-ramsay/another-note-on-party-memberships-in-uk

14. Peter Kellner, 'The problem of trust', YouGov, 13 November 2013. https://yougov.co.uk/news/2012/11/13/problem-trust/

15. As above.

16. Ali A. Rizvi, 'Seven things to consider before choosing sides in the Middle East conflict', Huffington Post, 28 July 2014. http://www.huffingtonpost.com/ali-a-rizvi/picking-a-side-in-israel-palestine_b_5602701.html

17. Akala–FireintheBooth.https://www.youtube.com/watch?v=sEOKgjoxoto

The selfish generation: anxiety and belonging in a digital world

Noel Hatch

What does 'local' mean when your laptop brings the shop window of an eBay trader closer to you than the independent clothes store down your high street? Who has a more multicultural experience, the kid going to school in Brick Lane, or the Shropshire gamer learning Minecraft with children from across the world?

Globalisation isn't a new phenomenon, but today its impact is critical. The internet has accelerated the trend towards total, immersive connectedness, influencing every aspect of our daily lives. This form of digital globalisation is breaking down geographic, cultural and economic borders; as more of us spend time online, our affinities become more complicated. This has its benefits, shifting our generation's norms, attitudes, and our beliefs about how we should organise and display solidarity. Some of us may feel more connected towards online friends in other countries than the people we physically live with. At the same time, the breakdown in geographic, economic and cultural borders means that anxiety proliferates. Many people feel a need for belonging that is not satisfied by global connectedness.

This kind of connectedness has pros and cons. It provides the means to crowdsource data to help cancer research, but on the other hand, we outsource production to 'digital sweatshops',[1] where people are paid pennies for menial tasks, such as comparing different web pages. Technology isn't just automating jobs, it's also making the need for many professions redundant – from assembly line workers to secretaries. At the same time, the internet provides us with the infrastructure to market, distribute and manufacture goods and services for next to nothing, and creates new jobs, from data scientists to digital makers.

While young people are faced with the challenges and opportunities of digital globalisation, the expectations we grew up with – being able to get a degree, a well-paid job, and ownership of a home – are unreachable for most of us. Fifty years ago, over two thirds of thirty-year-olds had attained these perceived markers of adulthood. Nowadays, those numbers have almost halved.[2]

At the same time, the welfare state – the social institution that played such a big role in helping our parents' generation achieve their aspirations – isn't helping people to cope, nor is it helping us to shape the changes we're experiencing. Jobcentres are more focused on keeping people off benefits than getting people into work. Schools are forced to focus on getting us into increasingly expensive universities, or training us for jobs that no longer exist. And housing benefits or equity loans barely cover even the lowest rents.

Social security's principles of solidarity don't fit in with the global digital era, which favours transactional reciprocity: 'I will (only) help you if you help me (first)'. This is exemplified by online systems where you build up points for doing good and can redeem them for prizes, like Bingo Giving. These systems function like an online currency exchange, turning acts of solidarity into economic transactions.

Recent research by Ipsos Mori shows that our generation are the least supportive of redistribution by the welfare state.[3] Perhaps the reason that institutionalised solidarity seems under threat is that our needs have often been expressed in such an individual way that it's difficult to connect them via an interface like the welfare state, which originally worked to bind people together against common 'social evils'.[4]

What's the point of a Jobcentre, when you're competing in real-time for a zero-hours contract? Who wants to use a benefits system when it rips off your last shreds of dignity, versus payday lenders who give you money with no questions asked? Who is social housing for when you're unlikely to stay in the area for more than a few years? With all of this, why would our generation invest emotional and political commitment in the welfare state, which we didn't help shape and which isn't working to make us more autonomous or equal?[5]

Even the idea of solidarity could even be seen to impinge on people's concept of individual freedom, not just the 'right to be forgotten' but the 'right to be indifferent'. We've grown up in a society which gives everyone 'human rights' to pursue their personal preferences. The flip-side is that we then see others as individually responsible for anything that happens to them.

These trends create brittleness in interpersonal trust, with less than half our generation saying that they would trust people they don't know.[6] This means we are more likely to perceive a lack of reciprocity with those we live or work with and, as such, we are dependent on weak interpersonal ties and create a risk of increased social tension. Such insecurity can give rise to fear. The more anxious we feel about our social position, the more we become what Agata Pyzik terms 'welfare chauvinists' – wanting to restrict the support given to those less well off. As she argues in *Poor but Sexy*, we can even end up believing that 'if you don't exploit, you'll be exploited'.[7]

Now that the internet and social media show us what people around the globe are achieving, constantly, in real time, digital globalisation increases our fear of falling off the social ladder, of the 'other' that we suppose is pushing us off it. While checking our updates on Facebook, we may be getting the collective wisdom of our friends on how the world works. But the algorithms that drive the way Facebook and other platforms work, mainly serve up content that already matches our tastes and our opinions. This tendency towards homogeneity creates 'safe bubbles', which, in lacking diversity, narrow down our outlook on the world.[8] In *Liquid Modernity*, theorist Zygmunt Bauman argues that the more people inhabit a safe bubble, free from divergent opinion, the 'more difficult it is to feel at home in the face of strangers, the more threatening the difference appears and the deeper and more intense is the anxiety it breeds'.[9]

Yet people are creating new forms of belonging and solidarity. The 'collaborative economy' blends modern digital tools with pre-capitalist practices like bartering. This enables people across the world to exchange goods, services and skills, be it a borrowed drill, somewhere to sleep or Mandarin lessons. By exchanging resources, we also build solidarity and even a sense of being part of a movement, whether that's with people in other countries, as with the 'couch surfing community' or with local people we didn't know had the same needs or interests.

But these initiatives have not been able to tackle the systemic issues that are causing economic disadvantage. You might be able to stay on someone's couch, but what happens if that person's house is repossessed? You might be able to grow your own food, but what happens when your allotment patch gets sold by the council for housing?

Though this kind of sharing economy has some radical potential, we shouldn't kid ourselves: it could be co-opted to reinforce digital globalisation's negative trends. In their description of the four scenarios of the collaborative economy, Vasillis Kotakis and Michel Bauwens describe how some of the most well-known examples of the sharing economy, like Kickstarter or Bitcoin, can actually reinforce one of the main inequalities driving economic insecurity – asset inequality.[10] Kickstarter, for example, allows companies to crowdfund the development of services, but the people doing the crowdfunding have no share in those services. Through limiting the amount of coins, Bitcoin induces behaviours that led early Bitcoin owners to hoard what they accumulated.

If those actors of the collaborative economy are able to co-opt our creative civic behaviours, then we need to build our own infrastructure which stewards the assets that are being shared and manages how they are shared. We need to share control of the projects we develop with those that take part in them, redistributing any surplus resources accumulated, and open sourcing the algorithms, business models and data that power these services.[11] Some initiatives, like knowledge commons, The P2P Foundation and community stewardship group Edgeryders are already active in this area.

The future of our society will be between an economy where our assets are co-opted, privatised and monopolised, and an economy where people co-create, co-invest and co-own common goods. As Buckminster Fuller has argued; 'You never change things by fighting the existing reality'.

Noel Hatch develops and manages research and design programmes for public services, think tanks and cultural organisations to better involve communities and transform services. He is passionate about social design, ethnographic research and systems change. Noel has co-founded various award-winning civic innovation and social design programmes, including Transformed by You, Creative Campaigns Camp and the Kent MBA Programme. Within European Alternatives, he runs the Making a Living, London Transeuropa Festival, Hack (y)Our Borders, Mapping the Civic Economy programmes. He is currently a Hub Launchpad Scholar, RSA Fellow and writer for New Start Mag.

Notes

1. Fiona Graham, 'Crowdsourcing work: Labour on demand or digital sweatshop?', BBC News, 22 October 2010. http://www.bbc.co.uk/news/business-11600902

2. Good Infographics – http://awesome.good.is/transparency/web/1206/the-generation-that-doesn-t-shut-down/flat.html

3. Ipsos Mori, http://www.ipsos-mori-generations.com/welfare (Accessed 2 March 2015)

4. Nicholas Timmins, 'Commission on social justice: Beveridge's appeal', *The Independent*, 25 October 1994. http://www.independent.co.uk/news/uk/commission-on-social-justice-beveridges-appeal-for-an-attack-on-five-giant-evils-the-beveridge-report-turned-its-author-into-a-hero-the-peoples-william-nicholas-timmins-reports-1444837.html

5. Ipsos Mori, http://www.ipsos-mori-generations.com/Pride-in-welfare-state (Accessed 2 March 2015)

6. Ipsos Mori, http://www.ipsos-mori-generations.com/Trust (Accessed 2 March 2015)

7. Agata Pyzik, *Poor but Sexy, Culture Clashes in Europe East and West*, London: 2014.

8. Francesco Carrollo, The Algorithmic Power that Shapes Our Lives, 22 August 2014. https://medium.com/@Innovandiamo/the-algorithmic-power-that-shape-our-lives-ad7ff2a7a353

9. Zygmunt Bauman, *Liquid Modernity*, London, 2000.

10. Vasilis Kostakis and Michel Bauwens, August 2014. http://p2pfoundation.net/Network_Society_and_Future_Scenarios_for_a_Collaborative_Economy

11. Simone Cicero, 'On Competition, Collaboration and Innovation design', 3 November 2014. http://meedabyte.com/2014/11/03/competitioncollaborationanddesign/

Who groks Spock? Emotion in the neoliberal market

Matthew Cheeseman

Any topic can be used to think seriously about the future, even science fiction. I'm not particularly a fan of *Star Trek*, but I was drawn to it by the phrase 'I grok Spock', which I encountered whilst reading about the 1960s. The words lodged in my mind and became a cipher for an approach to politics, a way of thinking about radical possibilities. Shortly before *Resist!* went to print, Leonard Nimoy, the actor most associated with Spock, died. His death doesn't change my argument, it gestures alongside the text, to the significance that death always seems to evoke.

As many will know, the original TV series *Star Trek* followed the crew of the starship Enterprise as they explored space, 'the final frontier'. Like other products of the 1960s there were many utopian aspects to the show, which included a peaceful constitutional republic (the Federation), an ethnically diverse, multicultural (albeit highly gendered) crew, effective technology, and a classless, post-scarcity, post-capitalist economy. These radical ideas seemed to diminish whenever the *Star Trek* franchise was re-exploited: in the 1980s as *The Next Generation*, 1990s as *Deep Space 9* and *Voyager* and more recently as a series of films which have re-imagined the initial crew as youthful cadets, embarking on their adventures for the first time.

This recent reboot has proved popular. *Star Trek* was the seventh highest grossing film of 2009, *Star Trek Into Darkness* the eleventh of 2013, and *Star Trek 3* will be released to huge fanfare in 2016 for the fiftieth anniversary of the original series. In the new films Kirk and Spock behave more like soldiers in an uncertain world of passion and discipline. They are stridently militaristic, perceiving themselves as besieged by intergalactic terrorism. *Into Darkness* was dedicated to 'our post-9/11 veterans with gratitude for their inspired service abroad and continued leadership at home'. Just as Batman has recently been recast as a capitalist fascist thug,[1] contemporary western anxieties are played out in the once-hopeful but now bleak and depressing twenty-third century. The screenwriter of the fiftieth anniversary film, J. D. Payne, says it will explore a moral dilemma: 'Where you could argue … that "this" is what you should do, and if you're advocating "this" then it's actually evil'.[2] These words would not seem out of place in the mouth of a Western military 'advisor' to the Middle East.

These new films diverge from the 1960s *Star Trek* via the plot mechanism of time travel, which creates a parallel universe in which the new films are set. The idealism of the 1960s, with its daring attempts to imagine an equal society without socio-economic problems, are therefore being slowly erased by our more pessimistic era, which does not believe in anything beyond capitalism. A more liberated fictional future is being rewritten by films which deliver relentless spectacle and make huge profits for their makers. Only one thing connects them to the past: Spock, or rather, the late Leonard Nimoy, who played 'Spock Prime', the same Spock who lived through 'the original' *Star Trek* and then travelled back in time to appear in these new films, alongside his younger self. His screen time is hauntological, a ghostly reminder of a lost, perhaps better future.

The old Spock, green-blooded and telepathic, was a famously complex character split between two distinct species, human and Vulcan. Spock identified with his Vulcan heritage, burying his turbulent human emotions and focusing on logic. This made for a long and prosperous career, both on the USS Enterprise and with the 1960s public, because his logic-obsessed demeanour appealed to many. If not revolutionary, Spock was seen as evolutionary, the next step, a natural son of the Age of Aquarius, who represented the coming social changes that many in the 1960s, especially in the wider, transatlantic youth culture, believed in. Spock physically and emotionally articulated the rebellion that many people felt. It was Spock who, in an episode titled *The Way To Eden*, sat down and jammed with space hippies on his Vulcan lute. He was an iconoclast: he looked different, spoke in a different way and was in control of his own destiny.

This faith in Spock is represented by a slogan seen on t-shirts and badges from the late 1960s: 'I grok Spock'. It was this phrase that drew me to thinking about *Star Trek* and contemporary youth politics. The verb 'grok' references another alien, Valentine Michael Smith, a character from Robert A. Heinlein's wildly successful 1961 novel, *Stranger in a Strange Land*. This book was a counter-cultural touchstone, largely for its free and easy attitude towards group sex and mysticism.

Valentine Michael Smith was an orphan human brought up by Martians. Like Spock, he didn't understand 'human' emotions like jealousy or desire: the implication being that these were social traits learnt on earth, rather than an essential part of the human condition. He was also telekinetic, suggesting that earth humans aren't using the full capacity of our brains, a cultural idea that is repeatedly returned to, as in Luc Besson's recent film *Lucy* (2014). The verb 'to grok' is Martian for instantly understanding the essence of something. Imagine the dry atmosphere of Mars, where water is precious and exalted. When drinking water it is absorbed into the body, its substance and essence co-mingles with the drinker as one. In the novel, just as Martians grok water, they can grok people, situations or ideas.

Within this lies the Gnostic ideal of knowledge without learning, of a spiritual communion which appealed to more and more young people as the 1960s developed. Grokking became a counter-cultural buzzword, a synonym for the generational sense that something was happening, a change was occurring, that there was a new dawn on the horizon. This same sense was captured by the (slightly tongue-in-cheek) slogan 'Never Trust Anyone Over Thirty' which indicated that if you weren't part of the generation, you could never grok 'it', even if you tried. Grokking was beyond reason. It was this contradiction, between the highly logical Spock and the intuitive grokking that struck me. It reminded me of neoliberalism, which pretends to be scientific and logical and yet appeals to people's emotions, values and desires.

In his provoking 1972 book *Towards Deep Subjectivity*, Roger Poole describes the international student movement of the 1960s and 1970s as a mass movement of Romantics, embracing nature in their rejection of social conformity, capitalism and language. They believed reason had failed the world and had made it a poorer place. If you didn't grok that, there was no point arguing about the present or the future. Rationality itself had been poisoned, society was sick, so it was necessary to confront it with a spectacular development of the self: individuals marching, sitting-in, occupying space and chanting poetry. Individuals found the confidence to be themselves together.

These identity politics changed the west and gave impetus to the movements for gay rights, feminism, and racial and ethnic liberation.

Respect, tolerance and space for difference was fought for and, in some contexts, secured. Situated within such a movement, the appeal of Spock makes sense: an alien respected, integral even, to mainstream, human society, an alien blind to prejudice, who makes his own mind up on evidence. It is no accident that homosexual fantasies were focused on his relationship with Captain James T. Kirk from the 1970s onwards. Slash fiction, indeed, draws its name from the slash separating the two in K/S erotic fan fiction.

While the west developed greater confidence 'to be' Spock as the 1970s and 1980s progressed, it was grokking that had the most impact on how we relate to each other. In the last *Radical Future* book, *Regeneration*,[3] I wrote about how the right to intoxication, a tenet of the western quest for freedom, has been monetised by neoliberal processes until it has become an obligatory search for punishment. The way many people, especially politicians, conceive of the world has similarly been monetised. Free trade and market forces are now routinely given as the only sensible way to conduct public life. Because of the emphasis placed on individual choice, society has been ceded to the market, which is now held to be the final arbiter of fairness, efficiency and 'rationality'. The market is everywhere, dealing with production, labour and 'services' such as water companies, the Royal Mail and the NHS. It is as if the 'invisible hand' of the marketplace has become sentient, attached to a brain capable of making decisions about the public good.

As I write this essay, thinking about invisible hands, I learn from the internet that Robert A. Heinlein had coined many words other than 'grok'. One is taken from the title of his 1942 short story *Waldo* which imagines a misanthrope, Waldo Farthingwaite-Jones, living in a satellite above earth, which is populated, in his account, by 'smooth apes'. Waldo is weak, unable to lift his head or even a spoon, and yet manages to perform many actions via a series of robotic telemanipulator claws. Since the story was written, such devices have been invented. They allow scientists to handle materials in remote locations and are known as waldos or waldo claws, from Heinlein's story. It struck me that the waldo claw is a much better metaphor for the action of the market in neoliberalism than Adam Smith's 'invisible hand'. A waldo has something behind it, operating from a distance. In neoliberalism's case it is perhaps not a misanthropic weakling living in a satellite, but certainly a set of ideas, an ideology that makes claims on human nature and 'common sense'. The hand of the market knows us, groks our situation and does what has to be done, a waldo claw with ideas of its own.

There are other echoes of neoliberal mutation present in the language we still use today, like twangs from Spock's Vulcan lute. The verb 'to grok' is retained in computer culture, where it means to know a programming language so thoroughly that one can inhabit its code. One of the most pervasive and durable slang terms, 'hip' represents generational identity more than any other. From an old drug term for opium – lying 'on the hip', smoking drugs in a stupor – to being cool and 'with it', the hip is how we linguistically inhabit our generational body, from hip-hop to hipster, from the world's most popular musical style to its most exalted state of consumerism. Hipsterism, indeed, evolved from consuming cultural products thought of as 'awesome' (surely the closest contemporary analogue to grokking).

Nowadays awesome, hip bodies grok code as automated claws operate the market. Consumerism has become a second nature, recognised as logical and scientific by the grokking way of knowing. We have internalised our helpful waldo manipulators who have married logic with desire. This is why it is so difficult to imagine the end of capitalism: such an act is now against nature itself.

There is an argument that claims that if we can construct this situation, so we can deconstruct it, and just take power out of the claws of the market. This is one of the reasons why I write, especially about popular culture: to reveal these hidden telemanipulators and demonstrate the extent of their complex grip, locatable in characters such as Spock and Valentine Michael Smith. But this analytical power requires concentrated thought and action, which is difficult to achieve in a climate designed to prevent just that.

This is the irony buried within this essay: we are so embedded in media, data and trivialities which are not trivialities, just like Spock and *Star Trek,* that we can't find the way out. So although today we are all a little more powerful in our individual identities, just like Spock, we can't stop grokking data, media and images. The constant bombardment serves to disrupt thought, space and rationality. This makes it very hard to wrestle with the claws.

Many activists and theorists placed hope in the internet as a tool for organising thought and action. While useful, it has not yet presented a social grammar capable of rerouting (or rebooting) society. Indeed, it seems, especially in the last few years, that the digital mutation is becoming all too fleshy and familiar. Numbers have never been more physical, from the super-complicated equations which manipulate the 'mood' of the market, to systems constantly noting the vibration of the psyche through clicks and keystrokes. If you are reading this text there are bound to be many models of you out there, selfies in clouds that will only grow in value the longer you stay alive and accumulate more browsing history, purchase information and sociometric data. This really is the contemporary manifestation of grokking, so real and tangible that it leaves a metallic taste in the mouth, the weight of data on our tongues, a film of pollution. This is most evident in cities, where the physical and digital move fastest, caught in a flow of fashion, predictive text and hashtags. We are in communion, grokking the moods of the market, mirroring the fluctuations in radiation from abstract finance. This sense is at its strongest in London, our capital of derivative ghosts.

That's why ghosts and madness have, in the last decades, proliferated. We may find inspiration in them, but we are frustrated by their cyclical recurrence. *Star Trek* is fated to perpetually 'reboot' on our screens, this time with added terrorists and violence, packaged to thrill and seduce. Counter-cultural Spock (RIP) now becomes part of the problem, a chimera capable of delivering the Vulcan nerve pinch. As I said, it is hard to be coherent, to 'make sense' when capitalism has invaded time, language and space.

Words drift from the count, become meaningless, feed repetitious thoughts producing more chatter and ink. In moneyed London, even the Occupy movement was out-of-place, displaced from the Stock Exchange to St. Pauls, where it stayed for an incredible 136 days. 136 days of encamped protest in the shadow of the City of London! And yet there was something ghostly even in this fortitude. Perhaps what is missing, or stolen, is the sense of communion, of collectivity, the generational confidence of grokking, of knowing and absorbing the inevitable other. Perhaps this is what we need to take back from the market.

There are some groups who have already done this. The 'terrorists' that are generated every day by the news provide plotlines for our rebooted science fiction stories. They use grokking. Fundamentalism gives some young people something the claws of consumerism can't provide: a sense of purpose and unity. A power that cuts through the

layers of media, data and endless reboots. Through the unlikely pen of
Robert A. Heinlein, we can imagine why young people might want to
teleport out to the Islamic State:

> Grok means to understand so thoroughly that the observer becomes
> a part of the observed – to merge, blend, intermarry, lose identity in
> group experience. It means almost everything that we mean by reli-
> gion, philosophy, and science – and it means as little to us (because
> of our Earthling assumptions) as colour means to a blind man.

Whatever its provenance, there is a thirst driving young people to feel
the heat here, a desire to live beyond the twenty-first-century, beyond
the grasp of the waldo claws. These are not logical processes, not
Vulcan motivations, but desires from the human side of Spock,
burning drives to eclipse the market masquerading as nature. Our
radical future must be built between two extremes, the savage market
of chrome and data and the desiring pit of militaristic heat and
fervour, both capable of erasing bodies, of turning them into ghosts,
living and dead.

It is never easy to construct something, argue over it, explore and
achieve consensus. A radical future must come from ideas, words and
action. And that, really, is the only conclusion: we must continue to
listen, read and discuss, plan and protest. We must understand the
power of grokking, expose and oppose and think about hidden powers.
We must speak the limits of our thought while at the same time not
be afraid to restate arguments or to find the same arguments and ideas
in other forms. We must experiment. We must reiterate and continue
to claim Spock, not only because others will reboot him, but because
we must think with what has been made. Only by doing so will we
create space to explore a future, to gesture towards a time when the
phrase 'Live Long And Prosper' can be spoken with meaning.

Matthew Cheeseman is a researcher and writer. He teaches at the
University of Sheffield, blogs at www.einekleine.com and publishes
The British Esperantist (which probably isn't what you think it might
be). In the future, he plans to write an exciting thriller about
GOSPLAN, the Soviet state planning agency. @eine on Twitter. I
would like to thank Florian Roithmayr, whose Platform residency at
Site Gallery led to this essay.

Notes

1. Dan Hassler-Forest, *Capitalist Superheroes: Caped Crusaders in the Neoliberal Age*, Zero Books, 2012.
2. *Star Trek 3* scriptwriter J. D. Payne speaking at the LDS Film Festival, quoted on trekcore.com http://trekcore.com/blog/2014/03/video-jd-payne-offers-hints-to-star-trek-3-plot-describes-moral-dilemma-for-enterprise-crew/.
3. Clare Coatman and Guy Shrubsole (eds), *Regeneration*, Lawrence and Wishart, 2012.